The Global Sporting Arms Race

Campus Library

Veerle De Bosscher, Jerry Bingham. Simon Shibli, Maarten van Bottenburg, Paul De Knop

The Global Sporting Arms Race
An International Comparative Study on
Sports Policy Factors Leading to International Sporting Success

Meyer & Meyer Sport

British Library Cataloguing in Publication Data
A catalogue record for this book is available from the British Library

Veerle De Bosscher, Jerry Bingham, Simon Shibli,
Maarten van Bottenburg, Paul De Knop

The Global Sporting Arms Race
An International Comparative Study on
Sports Policy Factors Leading to International Sporting Success

Oxford: Meyer & Meyer Sport (UK) Ltd., 2008
ISBN 978-1-84126-228-4

© 2008 by Meyer & Meyer Sport (UK) Ltd., Aachen, Adelaide, Auckland, Budapest,
Graz, Indianapolis, Johannesburg, New York,
Olten (CH), Oxford, Singapore, Toronto
Member of the World
Sport Publishers' Association (WSPA)
www.w-s-p-a.org

Printed and bound: FINIDR, s. r. o., Český Těšín
ISBN 978-1-84126-228-4
E-Mail: verlag@m-m-sports.com
www.m-m-sports.com

PREFACE

The SPLISS Consortium came together early in 2003 to compare and analyse sport structures, policy and performance in three nations – Belgium (Flanders), Netherlands and the UK. Aware that increasing sums were being spent on high performance sport across the world, we were concerned that there was no model for comparing the efficiency and effectiveness of such investments.

The study, which subsequently broadened out to include Canada, Italy, Norway and Belgium (Wallonia), could not have been completed without an extraordinary amount of assistance from a wide variety of individuals and institutions. Athletes, coaches and performance directors in different nations provided information on their personal circumstances and filled in lengthy questionnaires. Many other policy makers, high performance coordinators, and sports officials also gave freely of their time and provided valuable insights into their policies and programmes. We are most appreciative of all their help.

Our greatest thanks go to the dedicated researchers who joined this study from the other participating nations: David Legg (Canada); Berit Skirstad and Torkild Veraas (Norway); Alberto Madella and Lorenzo Di Bello (Italy) and Luc van de Putte and Thierry Zintz (Wallonia).

This book is aimed at sports professionals, academics and politicians seeking a better understanding of the factors that lead to international sporting success. We hope that readers will understand the complexity of this research and we invite them to share their comments with us – especially concerning the further development of this study.

The SPLISS Consortium, September 2006

The Consortium comprises:

Belgium (Flanders): Veerle De Bosscher & Paul De Knop, assisted by Sophie Daniëls
Netherlands: Maarten van Bottenburg, assisted by Bas Rijnen
United Kingdom: Jerry Bingham & Simon Shibli

RESEARCH TEAM BIOGRAPHIES

Flanders (Belgium)

Veerle de Bosscher, Sports Policies and Management – Vrije Universiteit Brussel – vdebossc@vub.ac.be

Veerle de Bosscher conducted her Ph.D. on this international comparative study. She is a research assistant at the faculty of Physical Education of the Vrije Universiteit Brussel Belgium, in the department of Sports Policies and Management (SBMA). She graduated in Physical Education (1994) and has subsequently completed two Master's degrees: one in sports management and one in training/coaching. Veerle lectures on courses related to sports policies and sports management at the VUB.

Paul de Knop, Sports Policies and Management – Vrije Universiteit Brussel - pdknop@pop.vub.ac.be

Paul De Knop has a Ph.D. in Physical Education at the Faculty of Physical Education of the Vrije Universiteit Brussel, Belgium. He graduated in leisure studies at the same university and achieved a Master's degree in Sports Sociology and Sports Management from the University of Leicester (UK). He is dean of the Faculty of Physical Education of the Vrije Universiteit Brussel, advisor to the Flemish minister of Sport, chairman of the board of BLOSO (the Flemish Sport Administrative Body) and also chairman of the RAGO (Council of the Community Education). Paul's teaching includes areas of sport management, sport sociology and sport policy.

United Kingdom

Jerry Bingham, UK Sport - jerry.bingham@uksport.gov.uk

Jerry Bingham joined UK Sport when it was established in January 1997 after working for seven years in the former GB Sports Council's Central Policy Unit, where he played a substantial role in the campaign for a National Lottery. Jerry manages UK Sport's research and ethics programmes, seeking to ensure that policy decisions are based on sound evidence. Major projects in which Jerry has been involved in recent years include a study of the sports development impact of the 2002 Commonwealth Games and the establishment of the Value of Sport Monitor, an online monitoring service of published research evidence on the contribution of sport to a range of social issues. One important new initiative is a longitudinal study of the values and attitudes of talented young athletes in the run-up to London 2012. Jerry has a background in local government and, in the early nineties, worked as a freelance sports reporter on the Independent on Sunday.

Simon Shibli, Sheffield Hallam University - s.shibli@shu.ac.uk
Simon Shibli is a Director of the Sport Industry Research Centre (SIRC) at Sheffield Hallam University, England. Simon is a graduate in Physical Education, Sport Science and Recreation Management from Loughborough University and also a qualified management accountant (ACMA). The SIRC team provide research and consultancy services to a range of clients such as national agencies, national and international governing bodies of sport and local authorities. SIRC has been involved in elite sport related work since 1997 and with UK Sport is one of the founding members of the SPLISS consortium.

The Netherlands
Maarten van Bottenburg, Mulier Institute – University of Utrecht
m.vanbottenburg@mulierinstituut.nl
Maarten van Bottenburg studied sociology at the University of Utrecht and Amsterdam in the Netherlands. In 1994 he obtained his Ph.D. in the social sciences with a thesis on the differential popularisation of sports. Since 2002, he has been the research director of W.J.H. Mulier Institute – Centre for Research on Sports in Society, a joint venture of the University of Amsterdam, University of Groningen, Tilburg University, and Utrecht University. In 2004, he was appointed professor of sociology of sport at Utrecht University and professor of sport business at Fontys University of Applied Sciences. Maarten has published several books and reports in the field of the sociology of sport and sports management.

Canada
David Legg, Department of Physical Education and Recreation
Mount Royal College, Canada - DLegg@mtroyal.ca
David Legg B.P.E. (McMaster), M.H.K. (Windsor), Ph.D. (Alberta) is the coordinator the Bachelor of Applied Business and Entrepreneurship – Sport and Recreation Applied Degree program at Mount Royal College in Calgary, Canada. As a volunteer David is currently the Director of Finance for the Canadian Paralympic Committee and Technical Officer for America's Paralympic Committee.

Italy

Alberto Madella, University of Firenze - almadell@tin.it

Alberto Madella was awarded his Ph.D. in the Methodology of Social Sciences at the University of Catania, where he also graduated in Political Sciences. He is Lecturer at the University of Florence, the University of San Marino and at University Institute of Motor Science (IUSM) in Rome. Alberto's research areas are in sport sociology and sport management. He has served as general secretary of the European Association for Sport Management (EASM) and is Vice-president of the European Network of Sports Sciences, Education and Employment (ENSSEE). Furthermore he is responsible for the coaches' curricula design for the Italian NOC.

Norway

Berit Skirstad

Norwegian School of Sport Sciences - berit.skirstad@nih.no

Berit Skirstad is Associate Professor at the Norwegian School of Sport Sciences in Oslo within the Section for Sport, Culture and Society. She is responsible for Sport Management studies. Furthermore, Berit is the president of the European Association for Sport Management (EASM)

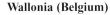

Wallonia (Belgium)

Luc van de Putte, Brussels European Sport Management Centre - Solvay Business School - Université Libre de Bruxelles - luc.vandeputte@ulb.ac.be

Thierry Zintz, Université catholique de Louvain (UCL) - Thierry.Zintz@uclouvain.be

Thierry Zintz has a Ph.D. in Physical Education at the Institute of Physical Education of the Université catholique de Louvain, Belgium. He is in charge of the „ETHIAS - Communauté française Chair in Management of Sport Organisations" at the Institute of Physical Education of the Université catholique de Louvain, Vice-president of the Belgian Olympic and Interfederal Committee , Deputy-secretary general of the European Observatory of Sport and Employment (EOSE) and also member of the Advisory Council of Sports (advising the Minister of Sport of the Communauté française de Belgique).Thierry's teaching includes areas of sport management and sport policy.

CONTENTS

LIST OF TABLES

LIST OF FIGURES

Chapter 1
Elite sports policies: An international comparative perspective

1.1   Rationale and problem definition

Over the last few decades the power struggle between nations to win medals in major international competitions has intensified. This has led to national sports organisations and governments throughout the world spending increasing sums of money on elite sport. In their quest for international success in a globalizing world, the elite sports systems of leading nations have become increasingly homogeneous. More than ever before, they are based around a single model of elite sports development with only slight variations (Oakley and Green 2001a, 2001b; Clumpner 1994; Krüger 1989).

The fundamental principle of what Oakley and Green (2001b op. cit) describe as 'a global sporting arms race' is that international sporting success can be produced by investing strategically in elite sport. Several nations have indeed shown that accelerated funding in elite sport can lead to an increase of medals won at the Olympics. Hogan and Norton (2000) even found a linear relationship between money spent and total medals won by Australia since the 1980s.

Nevertheless, in spite of increasing competition and the homogenisation of elite sports systems, the optimum strategy for delivering international success is still unclear. There is no model for comparing, and increasing, the efficiency and effectiveness of elite sport investment and management systems. This makes it difficult for sports managers and policy makers to prioritise and to make the right choices in elite sports policy.

The lack of an empirically-grounded, coherent theory on the factors determining international sporting success lies at the root of our research project. In the longer term, the main goal of this project is to increase our knowledge about the optimum strategy for delivering international success and the key performance indicators that demonstrate that an efficient and effective management of sporting excellence is in place. To start with, however, we have carried out an experimental pilot study in six sample nations to find out whether the data needed are available and comparable. Using the data we have collected, we present what might be learnt from theoretical, methodological and sports policy perspectives.

1.2 Establishment and organisation of the research project

At the end of 2002, a consortium of research groups from three nations initiated an international comparison of elite sports policy. Each of the research groups had already started a project of this kind in their home nation.

- In 1998, research on the elite sports climate had been conducted in the Netherlands, with the express intention of repeating this research every four years and using it as the basis for a potential international comparative survey. The research project was coordinated by Maarten van Bottenburg from the W.J.H. Mulier Institute, a centre for research on sports in society related to the universities of Utrecht, Tilburg, Amsterdam and Groningen.

- In the United Kingdom, an international elite sports index was constructed and a research project started, looking at how five European nations (France, Germany, Italy, the Netherlands and the United Kingdom) produced medal-winning elites capable of success in major international events. The research project was coordinated by Jerry Bingham from UK Sport and Chris Gratton and Simon Shibli from the Sport Industry Research Centre at Sheffield Hallam University.

- In Belgium (the Flemish part) a research project examining international success in tennis was started as part of a PhD study at the Vrije Universiteit Brussel. This international benchmark research focused on just one sport, namely tennis. Tennis experts from 21 different nations filled in a questionnaire on the policy factors that have the most significant bearing on international success in tennis. Furthermore data on tennis policies from 48 nations was collated in order to relate policy variables to actual performance in elite international tennis events and 15 tennis experts were subject to an interview on tennis policies in their nations. A method was devised to determine the relative success of nations, ensuring that socio-economic variables were taken into account. This research was led by Veerle De Bosscher and Paul De Knop from the Vrije Universiteit Brussel, Department of Sports Policy and Management - SBMA.

The objectives of the three research projects in these nations were very similar, though each one had its own specific focus and approach. In order to establish common ground, the first tasks of the research group were: to create an analytical framework for making cross-national comparisons in elite sport policy; establish the appropriate methodology; contact research groups from other nations; and to draft a research proposal. The common purpose of this project was reflected in the name "SPLISS", which stands for "Sports Policy factors Leading to International Sporting Success".

When the Belgian (Flemish), Dutch and English researchers began to disseminate the findings from their research, research groups from other nations expressed an interest in, and were invited to join, the research consortium. Ultimately, the pilot study is based on the three original partner nations and an additional three sample nations as detailed below.

- Norway: a research group led by Berit Skirstad, working with Torkild Veraas (a Master's student) from the Norwegian University of Sport and Physical Education in Oslo.
- Canada: a research group coordinated by David Legg from the Department of Physical Education and Recreation Mount Royal College in Calgary.
- Italy: a research group led by Alberto Madella from the University of Firenze, working with Lorenzo Di Bello (Masters student at the IUSM, University of Rome).
- In Belgium, the research was split into two parts[1]. The research for the French and German speaking community, Wallonia, was conducted by Luc van de Putte from the Brussels European Sport Management Centre and Solvay Business School. Additionally, information was gathered by Thierry Zintz from the department of physical education and physiotherapy from the Catholic university in Louvain La Neuve (UCL).

Researchers from a number of other nations (Australia, France, Germany, Greece, Japan, Portugal, Switzerland, Spain and Sweden) demonstrated a keen interest in joining the SPLISS project, but did not participate in this pilot stage, primarily due to a lack of resources.

1.3 Funding of the research

The financial constraints formed the greatest barrier to participation by other nations. There was plenty of interest, but in a number of nations the work done was largely dependent on the personal willingness and dedication of the researchers. In Norway the research was carried out as part of a Master's thesis at the Norwegian University of Sport and Physical Education. There was further assistance from Olympiatoppen who supplied general information on the athletes. Olympiatoppen also provided information about the elite sports policy and assisted with the circulation of questionnaires. Italy obtained logistical support from the Italian National Olympic Committee (CONI), via the Scuola dello Sport (an educational establishment for coaches), for gathering the data and the work of the secretariat. The research was carried out as part of a Master's thesis at the University of Rome.

Other participating research groups obtained funding for their part of the study in their own nation. In the United Kingdom the research project was financed by UK Sport; in the Netherlands by Netherlands' Olympic Committee*Netherlands' Sports Federation (NOC*NSF) and the Ministry of Health, Welfare & Sports (VWS); in Belgium by the Flemish Minister for Sports, the Minister for Sports for Wallonia and the Belgian Olympic and Interfederal Committee (BOIC); and in Canada by Sport Canada (a part of the Canadian Federal government within the Ministry of Cultural Affairs). In this initial phase of the project, no funding from international organisations was acquired. The costs of coordination and management were met mainly by the Vrije Universiteit Brussel as part of PhD funding, and by the other members of the consortium.

---

1 In Belgium the Flemish community (Flanders) and the French/German speaking community (Wallonia) have separate sport policies at each level, from local to national. Apart from the Olympic Committee (BOIC), whose main task is to select athletes for the Olympic Games, there is no national policy or structure for sport. Therefore Flanders and Wallonia have participated in this research as if they were two distinct nations. Brussels was included in both surveys according to the affiliation of the federations.

1.4 Objectives of the research

The objectives of the research programme were fourfold:
1. To compare and analyse data on sport structures, elite sports policy, the elite sports climate and the international sporting performance of the sample nations.
2. To conduct preliminary benchmarking of the sport policy factors leading to international sporting success.
3. To improve our theoretical understanding and methodological approach with respect to the identification of these key policy factors.
4. To inform policy makers and researchers from other nations about the SPLISS project to broaden the number of participating nations in this international comparative research project in the future.

1.5 Report structure

This research report provides an international comparison of six nations: Belgium (Flanders and Wallonia), Canada, Italy, the Netherlands, Norway, and the United Kingdom, and is structured as follows. Following this introductory chapter, we present in chapter two a classification of factors leading to international sporting success based on a comprehensive literature review, resulting in the identification of nine key sport policy factors, or "pillars". This is followed by a discussion of our research methodology and its limitations in chapter three.

In the fourth chapter, we examine various performance measurement methods, resulting in the presentation of an elite sport index based on 'market share' analysis. The purpose of this index is to be able to evaluate and compare the success of different nations objectively. In the fifth chapter, we present, compare and discuss data collected for the six sample nations on the nine identified pillars, namely:
1. financial support;
2. integrated approach to policy development;
3. participation in sport;
4. talent identification and development systems;
5. athletic and post career support;
6. training facilities;
7. coaching provision and coach development;
8. international competition; and
9. scientific research.

Criteria have been developed to compare and assess the data of the six sample nations. This in turn has led to the production of an 'at a glance' comparative analysis of each nation against each pillar. Where good practice has been identified it is highlighted and where nations have performed relatively poorly we have sought to offer explanations. It is important to point out that most of the data we have collected relate to 2004, with the financial data at Pillar 1 pertaining to 2003. However, elite sport is a fast-changing world, and we have sought to make it clear wherever we have provided more recent information.

The sixth and final chapter contains our conclusions which seek to explore the relationship between our assessment of the relative success of the sample nations and our analysis of their respective sports policy frameworks.

Chapter 2:
Theoretical model of factors determining international sporting success

2.1   Classification of factors leading to international sporting success

This pilot study was structured on the basis of a comprehensive literature review (See De Bosscher, De Knop & Van Bottenburg and Shibli, 2006). This literature review showed that there is a range of widely accepted factors which determine success in elite sport. To classify these factors, three levels were distinguished: the individual athletes and their close environment (micro-level), sports policies and politics (meso-level) and the social and cultural context people live in (macro-level).

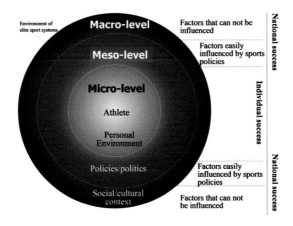

Figure 2.1: Model showing the relationship between factors determining individual and national success

At the micro-level we find those factors that influence the success of individual athletes, from genetic qualities to their immediate environment such as parents, friends, and coaches. At this level, some factors can be controlled (such as training techniques, tactics, psychological and medical support), whereas others, such as genetic make up, cannot be controlled. The macro-level contains factors like economic welfare, population size, geographic and climatic variation, etc. Several studies demonstrated that elite sports success is largely determined by macro level factors (Ball, 1972; Bernard & Busse, 2000; Grimes, Kelly & Rubin, 1974; Hoffmann, Ging & Ramasamy, 2001; Kiviaho & Mäkelä, 1978; Levine, 1974; Shaw & Pooley, 1976; Stamm & Lamprecht, 2001; Van Bottenburg, 2000; De Bosscher, De Knop & Heyndels, 2003a & b). However, a common characteristic of these factors is that they are largely outside the control of policy makers and political systems.

A consensus is building among researchers that macro level factors such as population and GDP are becoming less good predictors of nations' performance in elite sport than they have been historically. The principal reason for this view is that as nations become strategic in the way in which they produce elite athletes, they rely less on uncontrollable variables and more on the variables which are widely regarded as being the components of an elite sports development 'system' as argued by Oakley and Green (2001b). Australia is a good example of a nation which has recently been able to improve its performance in elite sport dramatically with (in relative terms) a modest increase in population. However, macro-level determinants still account for approximately 50% of Olympic success (Stamm and Lamprecht, 2001; De Bosscher et al., 2003a).

The middle level is called the meso-level. These factors are fully or partially determined by sports policies and politics. Elite athletes will have a greater chance of success, depending on the effectiveness of policy and the investment made in elite sport. In between the meso and the macro levels, there are other factors like media coverage, national sports traditions and anti-doping culture, that can have an impact on success, but where policy only has an indirect influence in the longer term. Within this classification, a further distinction can be made between factors that influence the personal success of an individual athlete and factors that influence the overall sporting success of a nation. This research focuses on the success of different nations.

Taking into account all the various factors that determine elite sports success, those at the meso-level are the only ones that can be influenced and changed. Surprisingly however, only a few studies have focused on organisational factors at this level. National sports organisations worldwide spend large sums of money in the quest for superior sport performance, although relatively little is known of the reason why some nations excel in specific sporting events. As it is our aim to create a framework containing a categorisation of policy areas that should be compared as drivers of international sporting success, an overview of literature at the meso level is provided. These studies can be classified into three types, which are reviewed in turn. The first type of studies are those focusing on a description of the organisational context of nations. Most of these surveys do not really compare the sports policies but rather simply describe them. In this way, plenty of research has been done on various aspects of developments in the former communist states (see for example Broom, 1986; Buggel, 1986; Riordan, 1989 & 1991; Sedlacek, Matousek, Holcek et al., 1994; Semotiuk, 1990). The former Eastern bloc nations have undoubtedly played an important role in the current developments of elite sport. As Houlihan (1997) notes, "nations like Australia and Canada have both adopted policies of elite squad development which are very close to the Soviet model in a number of key respects…" (1997, p6). This phenomenon can be illustrated by a general globalization process in sport. In this respect Oakley and Green (2001b) compared elite sport development systems in five nations: Australia, Canada, France, Spain and the United Kingdom. They discovered an increasing tendency to develop common strategies in those nations. However there is room for diversity and increasing variation (Green and Oakley, 2001). Digel (2001) compared the system of talent detection and talent development in China, Russia, United States, Italy and France. At the same time as the SPLISS project, a large scale research project on elite sports systems in eight nations – China, Russia, Italy, United States, United Kingdom, France, Austria and Germany (Digel et al 2003, 2004 & 2006). Although different in focus to the SPLISS project, Digel's study provides further insights into the operation of elite sport structures.

Recent research in the field of elite sport policies has been published by Green and Houlihan (2004 & 2005). They explored the process of elite sport policy change in three sports (swimming, athletics and yachting) and three nations (Canada, the United Kingdom and Australia). This study looks for similarities among the nations and offers in-depth analysis in four areas of elite sport policy: (1) development of elite level facilities, (2) emergence of 'full-time' athletes, (3) developments in coaching, sports science and sports medicine and (4) competition opportunities for elite level athletes. The authors concluded that:

> "despite all three nations being characterised as 'least centralised States', where we would expect to find considerable checks and balances to a dominant 'state presence' in a particular policy sector, federal/central governments in Australia, Canada and the U.K. have exerted considerable influence in promoting and shaping the values, organisation and activities of elite sport advocacy coalitions" (2005p 143).

A key characteristic of these studies is their search for similarities and differences among nations' elite sport systems. Although the underlying idea is to explain why some nations perform better than others, they do not provide pre-requisites for international success. This is the aim in the second type of study, of which there are only a few (Clumpner, 1994; Larose & Haggerty, 1996; Oakley & Green, 2001b). Larose and Haggerty (1996) used the innovative method of Ragin (1987) (Qualitative Comparative Analysis – QCA) to examine factors that contribute to international success. The authors found nine categories of important factors thought to determine success and presented these to fifteen Canadian experts, who concluded that a single model of factors leading to success does not exist. There was certainly no model that would cover all nations, nor one that would cover all sports. Clumpner (1994) used Broom's (1991) work as a foundation and suggested three major factors responsible for international success: (1) financial support for training centres and personnel, (2) an ongoing integrated Olympic Sport system and (3) athletic talent. Clumpner expands on these by identifying a range of other factors, including at the meso-level: time for training, well trained full-time coaches, sports medicine back up, international competition, early spotting of talent, access for all, a good communication network and an unbroken line up through the system.

Finally, Oakley and Green (2001b) identified ten items that could be regarded as uniform in the nations mentioned above, namely:

1. A clear understanding about the role of the different agencies involved and an effective communication network which maintains the system;
2. Simplicity of administration through common sporting and political boundaries;
3. An effective system for the statistical identification and monitoring of the progress of talented and elite athletes;
4. Provision of sports services to create an excellence culture in which all members of the team (athletes, coaches, managers, scientists) can interact with one another in a formal and informal way;
5. Well structured competitive programmes with ongoing international exposure;
6. Well developed and specific facilities with priority access for elite athletes;
7. The targeting of resources on a relatively small number of sports through identifying those that have a real chance of success at world level;
8. Comprehensive planning for each sports needs;
9. A recognition that developing excellence has costs, with appropriate funding for infrastructure and people; and
10. Lifestyle support and preparation for life after sport.

These three studies (Larose & Haggerty 1996, Clumpner 1994 and Oakley & Green 2001b) provide the foundation for an exploratory model of factors 'explaining' international sporting success. The authors conclude that further research is required to better understand "how" and "why" this tendency towards uniform elite sports systems occurs (2001, p.100). The SPLISS project is the first step in responding to this research challenge.

The third type of study focuses on the micro-level. The one crucial element missing in all of the previous attempts to model sport policy influences on success has been the involvement of athletes and coaches, as the key stakeholders responsible for delivering success in their nation. A number of researchers attempt to understand factors that influence the individual success of athletes, both positively and negatively (Conzelmann & Nagel, 2003; Duffy, Lyons, Moran et al., 2001; Gibbons, McConnel, Forster et. al., 2003; Greenleaf, Gould & Diefen, 2001; Nys, De Knop & De Bosscher, 2002; Unierzyski, Wielinski & Zhanel, 2003; Van Bottenburg, 2000).

In three broadly comparable studies at the micro-level level (Gibbons et al., 2003, Duffy et al., 2001, and De Knop, De Bosscher & Leblicq, 2004), an open-ended question was used to identify what athletes themselves considered to be the determinants of success. In all of these studies, the common theme is that the most important and necessary condition for success is the personal dedication and motivation of the athlete. Other consistently cited factors which can be categorised as 'an athlete's personal environment' include variables such as parents, partner and coach. At the meso-level, the quality of coaching exceeded all other factors. The importance of financial support, structural support and training opportunities, training facilities and competition appears in all studies. Therefore, from a policy perspective, support should be provided to maximise the influence of favourable personal factors. Having the talent, spirit and dedication are of course still essential in international elite sport, but factors at the meso-level are having an increasing impact on an individual athlete's chances of success.

Based on the previous research reviewed above, De Bosscher et al. (2006) concluded that the factors leading to success which are influenced by policy can be distilled down to nine key factors. These nine factors along with the notions of 'Input', 'Throughput' and 'Output' form the basis of the SPLISS analytical framework and are discussed according to these themes below. Inputs and outputs are clear. They can be expressed in quantitative or qualitative terms, and are, therefore, relatively easy to measure. Throughput refers to the efficiency of sports policies, that is, the optimum way that inputs can be managed to produce the required outputs. 'Throughput' is more difficult to measure and often will have to be assessed using indirect rather than direct means.

Input
Pillar 1 Financial support
Financial resources are measures of input, because nations that invest more in (elite) sport are able, in theory, to create more opportunities for athletes to train under ideal circumstances. As such, Pillar 1 is an effectiveness indicator of the input stage. Although a relationship between expenditure on elite sport and success (output) can only rarely be found in literature, there are many examples of nations that have performed better after increasing their investment in elite sport. This often happened after failure at important international events. As Chalip (1995) points out, these events 'focus' the attention of policy makers on proposals designed to improve performance in elite sport.

Throughput
Pillar 2 Integrated approach to policy development
The amount of resource devoted to elite sport is important, but it is the organisation and structure of sport in a particular nation and its relationship to society that enables efficient use of these resources to further the chances of elite sporting success (SIRC, 2002). There is no consensus or preference regarding the necessity for centralisation or a high level of government intervention in elite sports policies (Houlihan, 1997). As Clumpner (1994) notes, it is more important to have a good communication system and clear task descriptions. Furthermore, Oakley and Green (2001b) identify the importance of simplicity of administration through common sporting and political boundaries as another important item.

Pillar 3 Participation in sport
Although the relationship between sport for all and elite sport is often inconclusive, most top athletes originate from grass roots participation. Van Bottenburg (2003) found a significant correlation between mass participation and medals won during the Olympic Games (Barcelona and Sydney) especially when sport was 'intensive and competitive'. Similarly, at a sport specific level, a high correlation was found between the number of tennis players and international success in 40 nations (De Bosscher & De Knop, 2002). On the other hand, there are some contra-examples, like Australia's success in diving and cycling, two sports with a low participation base (Elphinson, 2004). We can state that a broad base of sport participation is not always a condition for success, but it may influence success to a large extent because it provides a supply of young talent and the opportunity for training and competing at various levels of ability.

Pillar 4 Talent identification and development system
Seen from a process perspective, Pillar 4 begins when a talented athlete is discovered and starts to receive special attention. It is particularly important in smaller nations that the highest possible number of prospective talented athletes is identified (Harre, 1982; Régnier, Salmela & Russel, 1993). Therefore, from a policy viewpoint, there is the necessity for: monitoring systems to identify talent characteristics; robust talent detection systems that minimise drop out; and well organised scouting systems (Rowe, 1994).

It is our view that, in most nations, talented athletes are recruited on a sport-specific basis, by the national governing bodies. Therefore, much of this aspect of international comparison needs to be studied in more depth on a sport-specific basis. Only a few nations have a generic talent identification system and these operate predominantly on a schools basis (such as the systems in the former Eastern bloc nations and those currently in use in Australia and China). The second phase of the pyramid is where the athlete follows a period of intensive training during which they develop a mastery of their sport. This is the phase of talent development. The evidence indicates that many nations have set up national coordinated programmes to support governing bodies to set up high level training and competition programmes and to support athletes to combine their academic career with a sports career.

Pillar 5 Athletic and post career support
The logical extension of the talent identification and development phase is the production of elite athletes capable of competing at the highest level. Many athletes who have the potential to reach the top drop out (De Smedt 2000). This pillar is often coordinated by national governing bodies or by elite sports clubs and therefore needs to be analysed to a large extent on a sport-specific basis. In only a few sports can athletes make a living from their earnings and pay for all the costs they incur. Therefore some nations provide financial support for athletes to meet their living costs and for support programmes to give them access to the services needed to help them realise their potential. Finally, athletes also need to be prepared for life after sport while they are still engaged in their athletic career.

Pillar 6 Training facilities
Four other pillars are present during the throughput stage, supporting the athlete during his/her entire career. Training facilities (Pillar 6) are an important success factor enabling athletes to train in a high quality environment. Facility provision also provides a link between participation and excellence. De Bosscher and De Knop (2002) showed that the number of tennis courts was highly correlated with international success of nations in tennis (r=0,858).

Pillar 7 Coaching provision and coach development
With regard to Pillar 7, the quality and quantity of coaches is important at each level of the sport development continuum. At the high-performance level, two criteria provide particular points of comparison in this respect. The first considers the quality and organisation of training certification systems. In some nations, like France and Australia, certification of coaches is required in sports clubs (López D'Amico, 2000). The second is concerned with the individual circumstances of (elite) coaches.

Pillar 8 (Inter)national competition
A coordinated approach to the staging of international events is the eighth identified indicator for successful elite sports policies. It has been shown in many studies on the Olympic Games that the organisation of international events in the home nation has a positive effect on international success (Bernard and Busse, 2000; Clarke, 2002; Johnson and Ali, 2002; Kuper and Sterken, 2001). Athletes performing in their home nation have the benefit of low travel costs and familiar weather conditions and facilities. In addition, the national competition structure is a significant criterion as competition is a necessary factor in player development (Crespo, Miley & Couraud, 2001). However, to a large extent the national competition structure needs to be analysed on a sport-specific basis.

Pillar 9 Scientific research
Scientific research (Pillar 9) concerns the systematic gathering and dissemination of scientific information in areas such as talent identification and development, medicine, nutrition, psychology, physiology and biomechanics. These factors were typical in the former communist nations and are key elements in the Australian Institute of Sport (Duffy, 2000).

Output
Throughputs can be seen as a measurement of efficiency of elite sport systems as they describe the way certain inputs may lead to the desired output. Outputs in elite sport can be clearly defined in terms of actual performance. Chapter four looks in depth at the different measurements of such outputs.

The SPLISS model
The relationship between the nine pillars and three stages of 'Input', 'Throughput' and 'Output' can be represented graphically as shown in Figure 2.2. The model presented starts with a focus on the athlete as central and then tries to conceptualise the following question:

"How should elite sports policies function so that elite athletes can train and perform in optimal circumstances at each stage of their careers, with access to good facilities, surrounded by high quality coaches and medical and paramedical support?"

CHAPTER 2

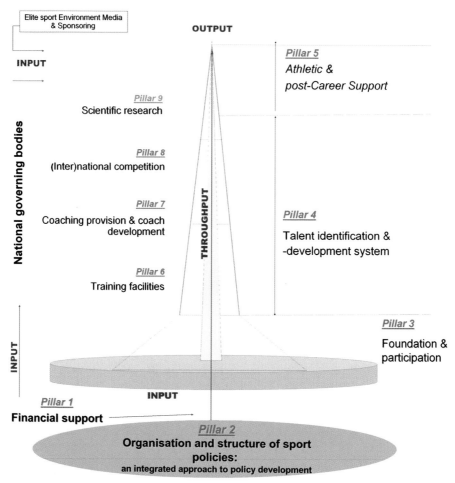

Figure 2.2: SPLISS analytical model

Source: De Bosscher et al. (2006)

Although the pillar framework aims to give a thorough overview of important sports policy determinants for international success, its function is not deterministic; rather it aims to generate the crucial questions that should be asked in a benchmark study of this type. This model may be subject to change over time. The model was tested in this SPLISS study in six nations, all recognised as "Western capitalist nations". It is possible that it would need to be adapted if applied to nations with different cultures (for example China or Russia), different sport systems (the United States) and at different stages of economic development (for example Kenya or Ethiopia).

The manner in which the research was operationalised in order to collate the data to make nation-specific assessments of the elite sports climate is discussed next in Chapter 3, Methodology.

Chapter 3:
Methodology

Terminology

Prior to outlining the methodology employed for this research, it is worth clarifying a few key terms in order to avoid confusion when making transnational comparisons. In addition to the three terms outlined below, other terms specific to the research are defined in the main body of the text.

National Olympic Committee (NOC)

The National Olympic Committee (NOC) for any given nation is the body recognised by the International Olympic Committee (IOC) to promote Olympism and to ensure that athletes from their respective nations attend the Olympic Games. Only an NOC is able to select and send teams and competitors for participation in the Olympic Games. Examples in the sample nations include the Belgium Olympic and Interfederal Committee (BOIC) and the British Olympic Association (BOA). NOCs are characterised by being recognised as bodies that are independent of government.

National Agencies for Sport

In addition to an NOC, whose work is often confined to the period immediately before and during the Olympic Games, many nations also have National Agencies for Sport (NAS). The typical role for a national agency for sport is to act as a lead organisation working in partnership with others to promote sport. In the UK, UK Sport is the lead body for the development of elite sport. Some nations also have 'umbrella' organisations for sport such as the Central Council for Physical Recreation (CCPR) in the UK. In other nations, for example the Netherlands, the National Olympic Committee and the umbrella organisation for sport (in this case the National Sports Federation) have merged to form a single body (NOC*NSF), responsible both for elite sport and sport for all and which is broadly comparable to the BOA and the CCPR in the UK. Whilst most nations have systems designed to perform homogenous functions, the structures by which these functions are delivered tend to be heterogeneous.

National Governing Body (NGB)

National Governing Bodies (NGBs) manage eligibility, rules and championships for individual sports within a given nation. Each National Governing Body sanctions competitions in its nation, and those competitions follow NGB rules. Typical examples of NGBs include Athletics Canada and the Flemish Gymnastics Federation. Other terms that mean the same are "National Sport Organisations" (NSO), often used in Canadian studies, and 'Sports Federations'.

3.1   Introduction

The nations involved in this research project can be divided into two discrete groups. First, those nations that are part of the SPLISS consortium, namely Belgium (Flanders), the Netherlands and the United Kingdom. Second, those nations that have contributed to the research but which are not formally part of the SPLISS consortium, namely Canada, Norway, Wallonia[2] and Italy.

Research data were collected in two ways.
First, all participating nations undertook to survey elite athletes, coaches and co-ordinators (Performance Directors), using written questionnaires, prior to the Athens Olympics in order to benchmark the 'elite sports climate' and to facilitate cross national comparisons on selected variables common to all surveys. What is meant by the term 'elite sports climate' is defined by Van Bottenburg (2000) as:

> The social and organisational environment that provides the circumstances in which athletes can develop into elite sports athletes and can continue to achieve at the highest levels in their branch of sport.

Second, researchers in each nation completed an extensive semi-structured questionnaire with open and closed questions on diverse aspects of nations' overall sport policies with particular reference to elite sport (and its evolution over the past ten years). This questionnaire was known as the 'Policy' questionnaire and contained 84 questions, the answers to which ran to in excess of 30 pages per nation. These questions, based on the nine pillars described in chapter two, mainly concerned the 'throughput process', and in particular the way in which sports policy is managed in each contributing nation.

The level of detail required to complete the Policy questionnaire was such that for each nation the task was a large scale research project in its own right. To answer many of the questions researchers had to analyse secondary sources and policy documents about elite sport policy in his or her own nation, they then had to undertake interviews with the National Olympic Committee and national agencies for sport and had to search for existing national surveys if required. This was a comprehensive task and with the limited resources for this survey in some nations, it was not always possible to collect sufficiently detailed information. Many questions had to be followed up or clarified at a later data by email or telephone in order to ensure standardisation of responses across the sample.

The open ended questions were mainly concerned with obtaining an insight into the policy system in each nation. Closed questions were added to ensure a degree of comparability on different sub-criteria. Each question left space for specific remarks and each pillar ended with two specific questions concerning: firstly, the main strengths and weaknesses of the findings from each pillar; and, second, suggestions for improvement in the opinion of the researcher. These open sections also provided an opportunity for researchers to give more details about possible additional criteria that were not included in our original questionnaires.

---

2   Flanders is the northern, Flemish speaking part of Belgium, Wallonia the southern, French and German speaking part. Because sport and elite sport is only organised at regional level in Belgium the research was conducted in Wallonia and Flanders.

3.2 Research protocol

In order to benchmark the elite sports climate and to facilitate cross national comparisons on selected variables common to all surveys, surveys were carried out in the six sample nations among elite sports athletes, elite sports coaches and elite sports coordinators (Performance Directors) of the national governing bodies for sport.

To ensure the reliability and comparability of the elite sports climate survey data, a research protocol was drafted, containing a description of methods to be used, definitions of the target groups, and guidelines for the sports to be included in the research. The definitions of the target groups were based on the pioneering work undertaken in the Netherlands in 1998. An 'elite athlete' was defined in this research as:

> An athlete who, as an individual or as part of a team, has participated in an elite sports discipline in a European Championship, World Championship, Olympic Games or other competitions that are comparable to these championships or games in the last twelve months.

An 'elite sports discipline' was defined as:

> A discipline that meets the IOC criteria or a minimum number of participating nations in the World Championships.

An 'elite coach' was defined as "a coach who trains elite athletes or talented youths". If no central register of elite coaches existed at a national level, the requisite data had to be collected separately on a sport-by-sport basis or via secondary analysis of National Governing Body and national sport agency records.

An 'elite sports coordinator' (Performance Director) for a national governing body of sport was defined as "the person who, within the federation (NGB) for a specific branch of sport, is responsible for elite sport."

Each nation also received three documents for each target group: a 'Word' template that could be used for the initial processing of the policy survey data in each nation; a pre-formatted data file configured in SPSS (the Statistical Package for the Social Sciences) into which returned surveys could be input; and an instruction manual to accompany the SPSS database, so as to avoid possible interpretative errors in the data analysis.

It was emphasised that the questionnaires should remain unchanged, wherever possible, to ensure consistency of data collection and comparison across the samples. Furthermore it was also recommended that surveys should be distributed to the athletes, coaches and Performance Directors at the same time. Questions could be added to the survey by individual nations, but not deleted. The targeted response rate was 30% which is a reasonable return for postal surveys. Finally, the data collection had to be completed prior to the Athens Olympics in 2004, to avoid the respondents being influenced by the results of this event. As Canada entered the research project at a relatively late stage, the majority of Canadian athletes returned the questionnaires after the Athens Olympic Games had finished. The results relating to Canadian athletes are therefore subject to this caveat.

3.3 Methodological limitations

It is worth noting at the outset that this research was experimental and opportunistic. In the Netherlands an elite sport climate survey had been conducted in 1998 and was repeated in 2002 with the express intention of using it as the basis for a potential international comparative survey. Similarly in the UK a survey had been conducted of elite athletes on the 'World Class Performance Programme' in 1999 and in 2003 a follow up survey was conducted. Because of the different agendas and the desire for time series comparability in both nations, in practice only a limited core of the surveys in the UK could be made comparable on a cross national basis.

Having defined what is meant by an elite athlete, an elite coach and an elite coordinator, the approach adopted in the Netherlands, Belgium, Canada[3] and Norway was to identify people who met these definitions and to send them a survey to complete. In Belgium, a list of athletes and coaches at this level did not exist and had to be created by contacting individual NGBs. For other nations these definitions caused problems, as they did not correspond to their target groupings or they did not have access to their names and addresses. In the UK for example, the population targeted was the 600 athletes (able bodied and disabled) who were registered as being members of UK Sport's World Class Performance Programme (WCPP) as of July 2003.

Whilst it is highly likely that all of the UK athletes met the definition above of being an elite athlete, it is also highly likely that there were considerable omissions. In 2004, beneath UK Sport's 'World Class' level, each of the four home nations ran its own sub-elite athlete development programme. It is quite likely that many of these athletes met the definition of 'elite athlete' given above but who nonetheless were excluded from the research as it was solely concerned with athletes on the WCPP. Clearly these sorts of issues have implications for the degree of like-for-like comparability across surveys. Respondents from the UK had been selected to be on an athlete support programme whereas in the case of the other nations the athlete respondents had competed at a minimum standard threshold but were not necessarily part of a formal elite athlete development programme. With regard to the coaches' survey, youth coaches were included in Italy and Flanders, whereas the other nations surveyed only coaches working with elite athletes.

A further area for consideration is that the survey results have been produced in three different languages. Three of the nations recorded their survey responses entirely in English; however Wallonia produced data in French, whilst data from Flanders and the Netherlands is in Dutch. For nations such as Norway and Italy the original survey was translated from Dutch to English and from English to Norwegian and Italian respectively. This creates only minimal problems when analysing purely quantitative data, assuming that the question is interpreted correctly. However, it does create difficulties in relation to the interpretation of any qualitative data collected.

---

3 In Canada „minimum participation to European championships", was replaced by a comparable event of this level: „Pan-American Games".

Almost all participating nations had to carry out the research with limited resources, which is indicative of the opportunistic nature of the research. This, in combination with the fact that the research project was highly dependent on the cooperation of sports authorities and National Olympic Committees, which had not necessarily commissioned the research, resulted in practical difficulties accessing all target groups (athletes, coaches, Performance Directors). In practice only Flanders, Wallonia, Canada and the Netherlands surveyed all three target groups. The UK researchers did not interview Performance Directors; the Italian researchers did not interview athletes or Performance Directors; and the Norwegian researchers did not interview coaches or Performance Directors. The Policy questionnaire was completed comprehensively by researchers in all six sample nations.

The survey research achieved an overall response rate of 30% of the target groups actually contacted. However, the response rate varied depending on the nation and target group. Where response rates were particularly low (e.g. among UK and Walloon coaches), the data are used only rarely in our analysis. In Canada the Ethics Committee stipulated that a formal consent form was required to be completed by all respondents in relation to the use of data in an international study. In the case of 30 respondents this form was not returned and these questionnaires could not, therefore, be included in the survey.

The response rate for athletes taking part in disability sports was relatively low overall, except in the United Kingdom, where this target group constituted a quarter of the responses. As was found in the UK sample, the characteristics of athletes with a disability are significantly different to those of able bodied athletes. In particular, athletes with a disability tend to be older than able bodied athletes and consequently have different lifestyle patterns such as being much less likely to be in education. These results can skew the sample relative to those nations with a lower representation of athletes with a disability.

Another point of difference is that in the Netherlands and Flanders approximately two thirds of surveyed athletes were athletes who compete in individual sports, whereas in Canada 46% of the athletes' sampled was drawn from team sports. In Wallonia, Norway and the United Kingdom the balance of respondents from individual sports was the most extreme with only 4%, 5% and 7% of athletes respectively coming from team sports. In all nations the majority of respondents were drawn from Olympic sports and the ratio of Olympic to non-Olympic sports ranged from 71% to 29% in the Netherlands to 98% to 2% in the UK. It is important to give these factors due consideration when undertaking comparative analysis of the data to enable accurate interpretation of the survey results. The parameters of each nation's elite sport programme would appear to differ considerably with varying proportions of Olympic and non-Olympic sports and a considerable difference in the number of sports surveyed.

In addition to the breakdown of the sample by nation and type of respondent, we include in appendix 1 a breakdown by sport for each respondent type and each nation. This more detailed analysis enables the differences in the number of sports supported and the differing composition of the samples to be seen at a glance. The number of different sports included in the sample is 82 and this varied greatly from nation to nation. Athletes from Norway were drawn from 18 different sports, whereas athletes from the Netherlands were drawn from 59 different sports. By contrast, 27 of the 29 sports represented in the UK sample are either Olympic or Paralympic sports / disciplines. It should always be borne in mind when conducting research of this type that athletes, coaches and Performance Directors are in a strong position to give valid views on the elite climate they experience in their own sport, but are not so well placed to comment on the climate in other sports. Nevertheless, these sports are, or were, targeted as priority sports in the sample nations and thus all need to be included to get an overall view on the elite sport climate. However, no comparisions are made on a sport by sport basis.

In terms of summer and winter Olympic sports, the overall sample includes only 37 athletes from winter sports, of which 24 are from the Netherlands. The remainder of the winter sport respondents are from Wallonia (nine), Flanders (two) and the UK (two). No athletes from winter sports were included in the responses received from Norway. The under representation of athletes from winter sports in the sample may have only a small influence on assessing the general elite sport climate. However, it must be taken into account when considering the success of these nations relative to the policies employed to generate success.

The tables below provide an overview of the respondent groups and the indicators. Where relevant, limitations regarding the sample groups are discussed. In the remainder of this report, results will be analysed primarily at headline level for each target group and only rarely will there be comparisons across target groups on a nation by nation basis.

3.4   The profile of the sample of athletes

The number of eligible elite athletes in each nation, their respective response rates and broad profile are shown in Tables 3.1 and 3.2

Table 3.1: Athletes' response rate by nation

Nation	Athletes	Respondents	Response Rate	Proportion of Total Sample
The Netherlands	1,238	421	34%	38.6%
UK	600	279	47%	25.6%
Flanders	326	140	43%	12.8%
Canada	825	132	16%	12.1%
Wallonia	154	63	41%	5.8%
Norway	95	55	58%	5.1%
Overall	3,238	1,090	34%	100%

The overall balance of the athletes' sample is weighted by the high absolute number of respondents from the Netherlands (421) and the UK (279). These two nations account for 64% of all athlete responses. The low response rate in Canada should also be taken into account when results are interpreted.

Table 3.2: Profile of athlete respondents

Nation	Male	Female	Olympic Sport	Non-Olympic Sport	Team Sport	Individual Sport	Disability Athletes
Canada	44%	56%	99%	1%	46%	54%	18%
Flanders	54%	46%	84%	16%	38%	62%	4%
Netherlands	57%	43%	71%	29%	31%	69%	7%
Norway	66%	34%	89%	11%	5%	95%	13%
UK	56%	44%	98%	2%	7%	93%	24%
Wallonia	73%	27%	86%	14%	4%	96%	0%

The athlete profiles have largely been discussed in section 3.3 above, but nonetheless Table 3.2 illustrates concisely the lack of homogeneity across the sample by gender, sport type and responses by athletes with a disability.

3.5 The profile of the sample of coaches

Five nations taking part in the survey conducted a survey of coaches working with elite level athletes. In total 253 responses were received from coaches and the sample and population details along with the response rate can be seen in Table 3.3.

Table 3.3: Coaches' response rate by nation

Nation	Total Coaches	Surveyed Coaches	Response Rate	Proportion of Total Sample
Flanders	233	119	51%	47%
Netherlands	221	62	28%	25%
Italy	50	32	64%	13%
UK	303	23	8%	9%
Wallonia	80	16	20%	6%
Total	887	253	29%	100%

The average response rate by coaches of 29% masks a considerable degree of variation. In Italy the majority of coaches (64%) were surveyed, whereas in the UK only 8% of coaches were reached. In the UK at the time of the survey there was no central register of coaches supporting the World Class Performance Programme. In order to reach coaches, the surveys were distributed at a conference for elite coaches that was attended by about 300 people. There was no opportunity for follow up as there would be with a postal or online survey and thus for these reasons the response rate from the UK was relatively low. Consequently, the results from coaches in the UK (8%) and in Wallonia (20%) have only rarely been used in the further evaluation throughout this report.

Comparative difficulties emerging from differences in language and format in the athletes' survey are equally applicable to the coaches' survey. Differing sample sizes are also evident within the coaches' surveys with respondent numbers ranging from 17 in Wallonia to 119 in Flanders. The data from Flanders therefore constitutes 44% of the coaches' sample. The broad nature of coaches in terms of gender, types of sport and whether or not they worked with disability athletes is shown in Table 3.4

Table 3.4: Profile of coach respondents

Nation	Male	Female	Olympic Sport	Non-Olympic Sport	Team Sport	Individual Sport	Disability Athletes
Flanders	89%	11%	91%	9%	21%	79%	3%
Italy	94%	6%	88%	12%	38%	62%	n/a
Netherlands	84%	16%	79%	21%	24%	76%	n/a
UK	96%	4%	86%	14%	n/a	n/a	24%
Wallonia	94%	6%	88%	12%	18%	82%	n/a

n/a: not available

The majority of the coaches involved in this survey represented Olympic sports, ranging from 79% of coaches in the Netherlands to 91% in Flanders. The number of coaches working on individual sports ranged from 62% in Italy to 82% in Wallonia. Only Flanders surveyed any coaches working with disabled athletes (3%).

The number of different sports included in this sample also varied greatly in line with large variance in the sample sizes for each nation. Coaches from Wallonia represented nine different sports whereas coaches from the Netherlands were drawn from 30 sports. Overall approximately 50 different sports are included in the overall coaches' sample.

3.6   The profile of the sample of Performance Directors

A total of 71 Performance Directors were surveyed as part of this research from four different nations as shown in Table 3.5.

Table 3.5: Profile of Performance Director respondents

Nation	Response	Olympic Sport	Non-Olympic Sport	Team Sport	Individual Sport	Disability Athletes
Canada	11/34	100%	0%	30%	70%	n/a
Flanders	26/26	85%	15%	15%	85%	4%
Netherlands	28/54	61%	39%	30%	70%	n/a
Wallonia	04/21	100%	0%	0%	100%	20%

n/a: not available

Sample sizes varied from six (Wallonia) to 28 Performance Directors from the Netherlands. A 100% response rate was reached in Flanders with the help of the Sports Administration, Bloso. Performance Directors representing Olympic sports varied from 61% in the Netherlands to 100% in both the Canada and the Wallonia samples. The number of Performance Directors focused on individual rather than team sports ranged from 70% to 100%. Representation from disability sport was minimal. Owing to the low number of responses from Performance Directors the results are used sparingly throughout the rest of the report.

3.7   The representativeness of the samples

To put the survey data into an overall context, the representativeness of the responses from each respondent group has been assessed as pragmatically as possible as shown in Table 3.6.

Table 3.6: The representativeness of the samples

Nation	Athletes	Coaches	Performance Directors
Canada	Unknown	N/A	Unknown
Flanders	Unknown	Broadly	Fully
Italy	N/A	Unknown	N/A
Netherlands	Broadly	Unknown	Broadly
Norway	Unknown	N/A	N/A
UK	Broadly	Unknown	N/A
Wallonia	Unknown	Unknown	Unknown

"Broadly" = where 50%+ of the sample has been interviewed OR the sample characteristics have been compared with the population parameters i.e. checked for non-response.
"Fully" = population survey.
N/A = not applicable, the nation concerned did not interview this particular group

The key point from Table 3.6 is that at best some samples are broadly representative of their populations and for the most part the representativeness of samples is unknown. Consequently the quantitative results discussed throughout this report should be regarded as being indicative rather than definitive.

3.8　Summary Points

The total data available sub-analysed by nation, respondent type, and known number of different sports is summarised in Table 3.7.

Table 3.7: Data summary in alphabetical order

Nation	Canada	Flanders	Italy	Netherlands	Norway	United Kingdom	Wallonia
Athletes	132	140	0	421	55	279	63
No. of Sports	Unknown	21	0	59	18	29	24
Coaches	0	119	32	62	0	23	17
No. of Sports	0	22	18	30	0	16	9
Coordinators	11	26	0	28	0	0	6
No. of Sports	Unknown	25	0	28	0	0	5

Despite the caveats about the representativeness of the samples discussed above, and bearing in mind that all six sample nations conducted lengthy policy surveys as well, it should be noted that the results of this research are based on over 1,400 individual surveys and more than 200 pages of policy questionnaires. In this regard the SPLISS project is one of the largest data collection exercises of its type ever conducted.

Despite its methodological limitations, the research should be regarded as an important step towards understanding the issues involved in making transnational comparisons of elite sport systems. The unique feature of the research is that in addition to measuring easily quantifiable variables such as inputs (e.g. money) and outputs (e.g. medals) it has also tried to assess the 'black box' of throughput both in terms of the existence of various system components and also the rating that athletes, coaches and Performance Directors gave to these system components.

Chapter 4:
Measuring the success of nations in elite sport

4.1 Introduction

This chapter is concerned with measuring the success of nations in elite sport competition and the efficiency of the production systems employed to produce medal winning elites. It is implicit throughout this report that the 'production' of successful elite athletes by nations is an output from a strategic planning process. Nations for whom sporting success is an important commit to strategic planning processes such as the World Class Programmes in the UK or Performance 2008 in the Netherlands.

The components of these and similar programmes across the world are becoming increasingly familiar and are documented in the emerging body of literature. Oakley and Green (2001a; 2001b) argue, along with Clumpner (1994), that the elite sports development systems of the UK, France, Spain, Canada, USA and Australia are becoming increasingly homogenous to the extent that they are based around a single model of elite sports development but each with slight variations on that model.

It follows that if nations are adopting a strategic approach to the production of elite athletes, then part of that process must be to evaluate the results achieved (outputs) relative to the resources invested (inputs). The notion of the 'process' approach to the production of medal winning elites and the implied imperative of measuring performance is illustrated in Figure 4.1.

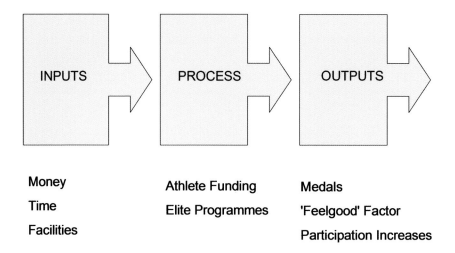

Figure 4.1: Elite athlete production as a process model

The aim of this chapter is to examine various methods by which the outputs of an elite athlete production system can be measured primarily using the Summer Olympic Games (28 sports and 35 disciplines) as a case study. Furthermore, we also examine the limitations of the analysis and propose some alternative measures that will need additional research in due course. The reason for including this analysis is that the key focus for the partners in the SPLISS project is to examine the effectiveness and efficiency of systems in order to identify who is performing well and why they are performing well. However, before examining performance measurement methods in more detail, we present an overview of the nature of the Summer Olympic Games.

4.2   The nature of the Summer Olympic Games

Along with the FIFA Football World Cup, the Summer Olympic Games is the most high profile event in the global sporting calendar. In recent editions of the Games the International Olympic Committee (IOC) has sought to make the event truly global. This point can in part be appreciated by looking at the number of nations taking part as shown in Figure 4.2.

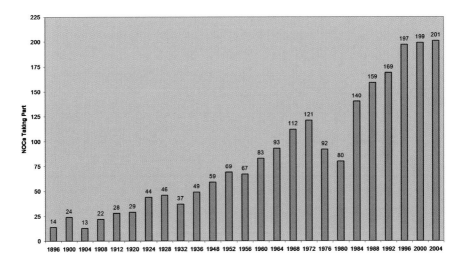

Figure 4.2: The number of nations taking part in the Olympic Games 1896 - 2004

Figure 4.2 shows that in the modern era (post Second World War), the number of National Olympic Committees (NOCs) taking part in the summer Olympic Games has increased from 59 in 1948 to 201 in 2004. Much of this growth has occurred since 1980 when the number of NOCs taking part in the Games was reduced as a result of the American led boycott of the Moscow Olympics. In 1980, 80 NOCs took part in the Games and there has been a steady increase in this figure to the record 201 NOCs taking part in Athens 2004 as shown in Figure 4.2.

As the number of nations taking part has increased, so too have the number of athletes, the number of sports and the number of events as shown in Figures 4.3, 4.4 and 4.5 respectively.

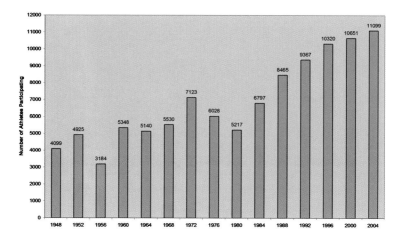

Figure 4.3: The number of athletes taking part in the Olympic Games 1948-2004

Figure 4.3 shows that the number of athletes taking part in the Olympic Games has more than doubled in the period 1980 (5,217 competitors) to 2004 (11,099 competitors).

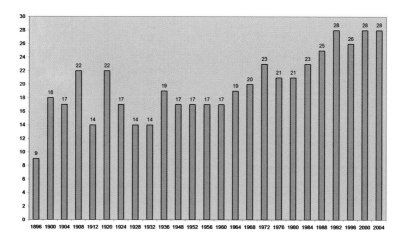

Figure 4.4: The number of sports contested at the Olympic Games 1896-2004

The number of sports contested at each Olympic Games has risen from 17 in 1948 to 28 in 1992, 2000 and 2004. Whilst a near 50% growth in the number of sports contested is in itself powerful evidence of the expansion of the Olympic Games, the increase in the number of events contested (121%) is an even greater testimony to the growth of the event as shown in Figure 4.5.

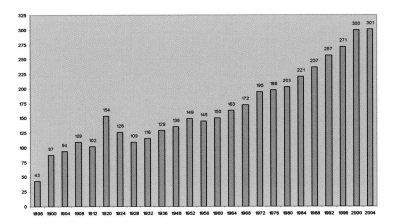

Figure 4.5: The growth in the number of events 1896-2004

The number of events peaked in 2004 at 301 and the long term growth trend in the number of events can in part be explained by two factors. First, the increase in the number of sports contested; and second, an expansion of the programmes for selected sports, notably an increase in the number of events contested by women athletes as shown in Figure 4.6.

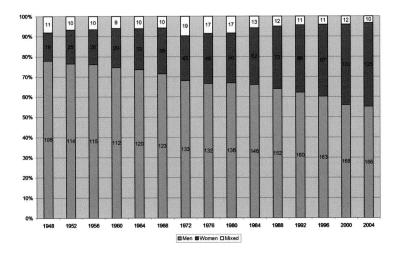

Figure 4.6: The number and proportion of events contested by women athletes 1948-2004

In 1948, 19 of the 137 events (14%) contested in the London Olympics were events for women only. If 'mixed' events are included in this total for 1948; i.e. events in which men and women compete together (e.g. badminton mixed doubles), or events in which men and women compete as equals (e.g. equestrian and some sailing events), then the number and proportion of events in which women could take part was 30 and 22% respectively. Fourteen editions of the summer Olympic Games later, in Athens 2004 women only events numbered 125, or 42% of the total contested. When 'mixed' events are included, women athletes were able to contest 135 events which equates to 45% of the entire programme. In short, 64% of the growth in the number of events contested in the Olympic Games between 1948 and 2004 can be attributed to the increase in the number of events for women.

An interesting finding from the data relating to increased numbers of nations, athletes, sports and events is that the number of nations that have developed medal winning capability has increased as shown in Figure 4.7.

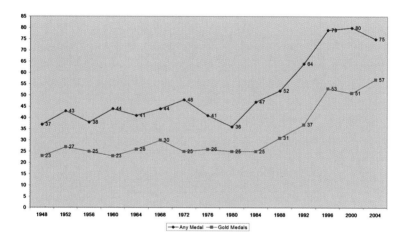

Figure 4.7: The number of nations winning medals in the Olympic Games 1948-2004

In 2004 a record 57 nations (28% of those taking part) won at least one gold medal and the number of nations winning at least one medal of any hue increased to a peak of 80 in 2000 (40% of those taking part). It could of course be argued that the number of nations winning medals has increased as a result of the increase in medal winning opportunities (Figure 4.5). However, further analysis of the Olympic medal table reveals that more successful nations are maintaining their medal table rankings despite winning proportionately fewer of the medals available. In 1988 the top ten nations achieved a market share (explained later in this chapter) of 74.5% and this fell to 56.9% in Athens 2004. It is our view that the reason for this fall is attributable to the share of success being distributed more widely, that is, more nations are developing medal winning capability. If more nations have developed medal winning capability as shown in Figure 4.7, then it follows that medals must be even harder to win and competition to win them must therefore have increased. The view that the Olympic Games have become increasingly competitive is an important contextual point and we develop the argument further in Section 4.3.

4.3   Evidence of increasing competition?

The trends shown in Figure 4.7, particularly in the post-1980 period are not a coincidence, rather the results of a deliberate campaign by the IOC 'to achieve a real universality' (Rogge, 2002). What is meant by the term 'a real universality' is for the Olympic Games to be relevant to all of the nations in the world. The goal of 'real universality' can in part be achieved by encouraging as many of the world's nations as possible to have an NOC and to bring a delegation to each Olympic Games. In 2004 this goal was almost met in full as 201 NOCs attended the Games out of a total of 202 recognised NOCs.

There are a number of factors that are attributed to the increasing number of NOCs that have developed medal winning capability. These can be divided into two distinct categories: first, factors attributable to an increase in demand for success in elite sport; and, second, factors attributable to manipulating the supply of success. The demand side factors are in part covered by Oakley and Green (2001a, 2001b) who describe the increased demand for sporting success as a 'global sporting arms race'. The term 'global sporting arms race' is an appropriate description of international sport at elite level because it conveys an image of a battle for sporting supremacy with no absolute goal, only the relative goal of staying ahead of the competition. Three demand side factors have been identified and these are developed below. First, new nations, for example those arising from the break up of the former Union of Soviet Socialist Republics (USSR), have used sporting success as a means of establishing their national identity. Since 1990, 30 new nations have been recognised[4], 15 of which relate to the former Soviet Union. The USSR competed as a single NOC (URS) from 1952 to 1988 and as 15 NOCs in 1996 (in 1992 URS competed as a unified team EUN). At the 2004 Athens Olympics 10 of the 15 NOCs that previously comprised the Soviet Union won at least one medal. Furthermore, in 2000 and 2004 the aggregate total of medals won by the 15 nations that previously comprised URS was greater than the URS achieved on its own when it last competed as a single entity in Seoul 1988, as shown below.

Table 4.1: Medals won by former Soviet Union (USSR) nations 1988-2004

		Gold	Silver	Bronze	Total
1988	URS	55	31	46	132
1992	EUN	45	38	29	112
1996	15 Separate NOCs	40	38	45	123
2000	15 Separate NOCs	48	48	67	163
2004	15 Separate NOCs	45	52	65	162

In 1988 URS won 132 medals whereas in 2000 and 2004 the 15 NOCs that previously comprised URS won 163 and 162 medals respectively. This growth cannot be explained entirely by the growth in medal winning opportunities, as the number of events contested increased by 44 (17%) and the number of medals won increased by 31 (23%). Although, as will be demonstrated in Section 4.4, total medals won is not the most robust measure of performance, the analysis above is useful in illustrating that an increased number of nations have medal winning capacity and that this is a recent phenomenon.

---

4   http://geography.about.com/cs/nations/a/newnations.htm

On a smaller scale the former Yugoslavia (one NOC) is now made up of five sovereign states which all have a recognised NOC. In the four summer Olympic Games from 1992 to 2004 a minimum of two and a maximum of three nations that were formerly part of Yugoslavia won at least one medal. Of the 30 new nations that have been recognised since 1990, 22 have won at least one medal in the four summer Olympic Games held since 1992. It is therefore reasonable to conclude that the summer Olympic Games have become increasingly competitive and thus medals have become relatively harder to win.

The relationship between the number of NOCs taking part in the Olympic Games and the number winning a medal of any type has been tested using regression analysis and produces a strong positive correlation (0.89) between the two variables as shown in Figure 4.8 below.

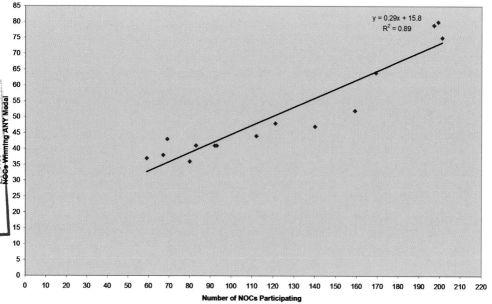

Figure 4.8: Correlation between NOCs taking part and NOCs winning at least one medal

In Figure 4.8 it is worth noting that in the last three summer Olympic Games (1996, 197 NOCs; 2000, 199 NOCs; and 2004, 201 NOCs), i.e. the period after the break-ups of the Soviet Union and Yugoslavia, the plots of NOCs winning any medal against the number of NOCs taking part are above the trend line. This means that the actual number of different nations winning a medal in these editions was greater than would have been predicted on the basis of historical data. This finding would therefore support the suggestion that competition for medals has increased recently, and as a result, medals are relatively more difficult to win.

Second, as a direct response to increased competition, some nations (notably those with a tradition of international sporting success) have seen their share of international sporting success reduced. The United Kingdom which won a single gold medal in 1996 and fell to 36th place in the medal table is a spectacular example of this phenomenon. To contextualise the scale of this decline in achievement, in the period 1948 to 1992 the United Kingdom had consistently been placed between 8th to 18th in the medal table for the summer Olympic Games. Chalip (1995) states that changes in policy follow what he calls focusing events which are 'nationally traumatic events that can symbolise an issue and focus policy makers' attention on proposals to redress the issue'. Some 'focusing events' in national sporting performance have led to massive investment in elite sport, often as a means of overcoming perceived failures. The dramatic change of policy towards elite sport in the UK can be appreciated by comparing policy in the early 1980s with that of the late 1990s following the 'focusing event' of Atlanta. In the 1982 GB Sport Council's strategy document 'Sport in the Community.... The Next Ten Years' stated:

> 'The Council will continue to emphasise excellence and to encourage it in numerous ways, but sees its role mainly in the better use of proven approaches rather than seeking any major new actions. Some nations invest vast public funds in special facilities, training programmes and financial and status rewards for elite athletes, in order to win prestige and trade internationally. It is neither tradition, nor policy to treat top level sport in this way in Britain.'

Following Atlanta 1996, the UK Sport Council was established with a remit for elite sport. The rules regarding the distribution of National Lottery proceeds were changed to permit certain types of revenue funding, notably grants to elite athletes to help defray their living and sporting costs. Furthermore, National Governing Bodies (NGBs) of 'priority sports' in the UK were able to apply for revenue funding to support World Class Performance Plans (WCPP). These plans provide access to world class coaches, sports science and sports medicine, specialist training facilities, and international competition. These are precisely the services about which the Great Britain Sports Council wrote in 1982: "It is neither tradition, nor policy to treat top level sport in this way in Britain." In the run up to Athens 2004, UK Sport invested £84m (National Audit Office, 2005) in personal awards to Olympic and Paralympic athletes and revenue funding of World Class Performance Programmes. On average UK Sport invested £21m per year in elite sport during the Athens Olympiad, a figure which equated to 10%-14% of National Lottery funds to sport depending on the level of ticket sales during the period.

The Netherlands has invested heavily in elite sport following the merger of the National Olympic Committee and National Sports Federation in 1993 to create NOC*NSF. De Knop, De Bosscher, Van Bottenburg & Leblicq (2004) report that the budget for elite sport in the Netherlands was €25m in 2003 and that this represented just over 29% of all central government funding for sport (€87m). Between 1998 and 2002 the central government budget for sport in the Netherlands was doubled to €75m. This increase in investment in the Netherlands was in part also driven by perceived failure. In the Winter Olympic Games of Albertville 1992 and Lillehammer 1994, Dutch athletes won four medals on each occasion. This level of achievement compared unfavourably with Calgary 1988 (7 medals) and Nagano 1988 (11 medals) and could be viewed as 'focusing events' for elite sport in the Netherlands. Achievement in other popular sports in the Netherlands such as football, and cycling was also disappointing in 1994 and in response to what was regarded as being systematic weaknesses in the elite sport system complaints about the system were voiced loudly in public. These complaints led the state-secretary of sport in 1995 to organise several round-table-conferences on the elite sport climate in the Netherlands which in turn led to more support for investment in elite sport from the sport and political communities as well as from the population generally.

Major investment and / or rationalisation of elite sport following 'focusing events' have also taken place in Canada, the USA, France and Spain (Oakley and Green 2001b op. cit.). Thus in addition to more nations increasing the competition for elite sport success, the response of nations seeking to preserve or enhance their status has led to a further escalation of the 'global sporting arms race'.

Third, politicians have realised and sought to capitalise on the potential of sporting success via the media platform that elite sport provides internally and externally. Internally, success in sport can help to develop national pride and to create a national 'feel good' factor. By contrast, failure can have the opposite effect. Thus politicians may invest in elite sport to achieve the former and to avoid the latter.

Success creates heroes and role models who serve a wider purpose for governments. Such heroes and role models act as an inspiration to up and coming athletes and may help to encourage the next generation of emerging talent. In addition, governments may have a wider agenda for sport whether it be seeking health benefits via increased participation in sport, or social benefits via the use of sport as a vehicle to promote social inclusion and equity. In these circumstances, the association of national sporting role models with government policy is considered to be a positive attribute for the policy initiative concerned.

Externally, there is a view that international sporting success can enhance a nation's reputation abroad which in turn may lead to improved political and trading opportunities. An increased number of nations have realised and sought to benefit from the internal and external opportunities of international sporting success, thereby contributing further to the 'global sporting arms race'.

In addition to its desire to create 'a real universality', the IOC is also actively engaged with trying to 'bridge the North / South gap' (Rogge 2002 op. cit.). The term 'North / South gap' is a reference to the dominance of Northern Hemisphere nations in both the summer and winter Olympic Games. It can be argued that the IOC has manipulated the supply of success in order to achieve its broader aims. To substantiate this claim, three examples are discussed below which provide evidence that qualification rules, the selection of sports and rule changes have had the effect of limiting the opportunities for some nations to dominate the Olympic Games and simultaneously increased the opportunity for other (arguably less dominant) nations to win medals.

Qualification rules ration the number of athletes from any NOC taking part in a particular event. For example in the case of athletics the qualification rules state:

> "Individual events - An NOC may enter a maximum of 3 qualified athletes in each individual event if all the entered athletes meet the A qualification standard for the respective event, or 1 athlete per event if they have met the B standard only."[5]

The net effect of rationing the number of athletes per NOC who can take part in an event reduces in part the effect of population. The USA with a population of 296m can only qualify the same number of athletes to the 100m as the United Kingdom (population 60m). If qualification was decided on the basis of absolute merit, for example the fastest 40 athletes in the last year, then

---

5   http://www.athens2004.com/en/AthleticsQualifications

the likely impact would be a raising of qualification standards and event dominance by a relatively small number of nations. Whilst absolute merit might be the most equitable way of allocating places from an athlete's perspective, the impacts of such an approach would be contrary to the IOC's aims of 'achieving a real universality' and 'bridging the North / South gap'.

The IOC also ration the number of nations from any given continent taking part in certain events by using a continental quota system whereby a specified number of athletes from a given continent are allowed to qualify for the Olympic Games as shown in Table 4.2 below.

Table 4.2: Olympic Games - Boxing Qualification Quotas

Classification	Africa	Asia	Europe	America	Oceania	Total
Light Fly	6	7	8	6	1	28
Fly	6	7	8	6	1	28
Bantam	6	7	8	6	1	28
Feather	6	7	8	6	1	28
Light	6	6	9	6	1	28
Light Welter	6	6	9	6	1	28
Welter	6	6	9	6	1	28
Middle	6	6	9	6	1	28
Light Heavy	6	6	9	6	1	28
Heavy	3	2	7	3	1	16
Super Heavy	3	2	7	3	1	16
Total qualifiers	60	62	91	60	11	284

[Source: http://www.athens2004.com/en/BoxingQualifications]

In addition to the continental quotas shown in Table 4.2, a further IOC rule in boxing is that each NOC is permitted to enter only one boxer per weight category. As there are four medals awarded in each weight category (losing semi-finalists both receive a bronze medal), then it follows that in each weight category four different NOCs will win a medal and therefore the supply of success is distributed more widely than would be the case if qualification was based on absolute merit i.e. if a dominant boxing nation like Cuba could enter more than one boxer per weight category. Currently there are 11 boxing events in the Olympic Games and therefore 44 medals to be won. Thus the most medals any nation could win in boxing is 11 and, as in Figure 4.7 (see earlier), the number of different nations winning medals for boxing exhibits a similar upward trend.

Oakley and Green (2001b op. cit.) state that there is a distinct 'western' bias in the portfolio of sports contested at the Olympic Games. This, they argue, ignores the sporting traditions of some nations and therefore puts such nations at a disadvantage. Much of the growth in the number of different sports contested in the summer Olympic Games can be attributed to attempts to achieve an improved 'cultural balance' in the sports contested. For example, the re-introduction of archery in 1972 has enabled nations such as Korea, China, Indonesia and Taipei to win medals. Similarly, the introduction of table tennis in 1988 and badminton in 1992 has made the Olympic Games relevant to huge viewing audiences (or markets) in the Far East. Korea's consistent performance in archery, badminton and table tennis is such that it has been placed higher than the United Kingdom in all but one (2000) of the summer Olympic Games since 1984. Interestingly, Korea has a population of 48m compared with 60m in the UK. Measures such as the cultural balancing of sports contested are consistent with the aims of 'a real universality' and bridging 'the North / South gap'.

Rule changes in certain sports have created conditions whereby a greater number of nations have been able to win medals. A notable example is judo which was introduced as an Olympic sport in Tokyo, 1964. At the Tokyo Olympics, four judo events were contested and twelve medals i.e. three per event were awarded. When judo was re-introduced to the Olympic programme in 1972, there were six events and a second bronze medal was contested by those fighters who were eliminated by eventual semi-finalists via a repêchage competition. As in the case of boxing, the qualification rules for judo are such that each NOC can enter only one athlete per event. Thus, as is also the case in boxing, it is guaranteed that four different NOCs will win a medal in each weight category. An identical situation takes place in the sport of taekwando, which was first contested in the Seoul Olympics of 1988 and is further evidence of a policy designed to distribute success widely rather than to permit dominance by a few nations.

In addition to the factors relating to the demand for and supply of success in the Olympic Games, there is an additional factor which has led to an increase in the number of nations developing medal winning capability, namely the increased ease of nationality change. Whilst nationality change is nothing new, the United Kingdom hastily provided the former and now current South African Zola Budd with UK citizenship to enable her to compete for GBR in the 1984 Olympic Games. More recently there has been a 'talent drain' from Kenya via the change of nationalities of Stephen Cherono (Qatar), Wilson Kipketer (Denmark) and Bernard Lagatt (USA). Nationality change is likely to remain an influential factor in determining the number of NOCs with medal winning capability. The maximum qualification period for an athlete changing nationality is three years and this period can be reduced to one year if both the current and prospective NOCs support such a change. For some nations, particularly those wishing to derive the potential benefits of international sporting success discussed above, 'purchasing' talent via nationality change may well be a more cost effective and time efficient approach than setting up their own talent confirmation and development programmes.

As the supply of medals (success) remains essentially fixed (the IOC has indicated that it would like the number of events to be capped at around 300), and demand for success increasing (more nations taking part and more nations winning medals), then the 'market' adjusts by raising the 'price of success'. In practice, an increase in the 'price of success' means that even more resources need to be invested in order for a nation to retain its medal winning capability. This point has two important implications for assessing performance. First, if the view that there is a 'global sporting arms race' in elite sport is accepted, then it follows that if a nation is able to maintain its level of performance in an environment of increased competition, then the nation concerned must have improved simply to keep pace with the competition. Second, if at any point a nation disengages from the 'global sporting arms race', then all things being equal, it will expect to see a deterioration in performance as it loses ground to competitor nations that have continued to invest in the development of medal winning elites.

As a consequence of investing increasing resources in pursuit of elite sport success, the need for performance appraisal increases so that those providing the resources to fund success can derive some feedback on their return on investment. We now proceed to explain how performance can be measured in the Olympic Games so that objective criteria can be used to diagnose how a given NOC is performing and how 'success' can be identified.

4.4   Measuring performance in the Olympic Games

This section is based on a research project carried out for UK Sport by the Sport Industry Research Centre at Sheffield Hallam University (UK Sport, 2003). The original research focussed on performance in the Summer Olympic Games 1948 - 2000 and has been updated to include the additional findings of Athens 2004. Although the examples used throughout this section are predominantly based on the UK, the Netherlands and Belgium, the basic principles are applicable to all nations that take a strategic approach to the development of elite athletes. Whilst it would have been relatively straight forward to include the same analysis for other nations, in the interests of brevity we focus primarily on the key partners in the SPLISS project. The IOC does not recognise the Olympic medal table as an order of merit. Nonetheless, it is widely accepted outside of the IOC that the final medal table for each games is an order of merit. This finding is perhaps best demonstrated by the fact that many nations invest heavily in sport precisely to climb the unofficial order of merit. Despite the medal table's simplicity of being a list in descending order of gold, silver and bronze medals, it is not an effective measure of performance for a number of reasons. To illustrate these reasons, an excerpt from the Athens 2004 games is reproduced below in Table 4.3.

Table 4.3: Excerpt from Athens 2004 medal table (a)

Nation	Gold	Silver	Bronze	Medals
1. United States of America USA	35	40	28	103
2. People's Republic of China CHN	32	17	14	63
3. Russian Federation RUS	27	27	38	92
4. Australia AUS	17	16	16	49
5. Japan JAP	16	9	12	37
6. Germany GER	14	16	19	49
7. France FRA	11	9	13	33
8. Italy ITA	10	11	11	32
9. Korea KOR	9	12	9	30
10. Great Britain GBR	9	9	12	30
17. Norway NOR	5	0	1	6
18. Netherlands NED	4	9	9	22
21. Canada CAN	3	6	3	12
51. Belgium BEL	1	0	2	3

The first key weakness with the medal table is that it is a measure of relative rather than absolute achievement because it uses a partial ordinal scale of measurement. For example, in Athens 2004 the USA achieved first place with 35 gold medals which is three more than China in second place; whereas Russia achieved third place with 27 gold medals which is ten more than Australia in fourth place. In addition to the medal table giving no detail on the absolute difference between places, it is also possible for nations to improve their position in the ranking table simply by other nations performing less well. This point can be illustrated through an extreme example. If there are 301 events contested in Beijing 2008 and China won 300 gold medals and Great Britain and Northern Ireland won one gold medal, then China would be placed first in the table and Great Britain and Northern Ireland would be placed second. It would be difficult for UK Sport to make the case that Great Britain and Northern Ireland had improved from 10th to 2nd in the medal table whilst at the same time achieving eight gold medals fewer than in Athens 2004. In short, a fundamental weakness of the Olympic medal table is that it is possible for the ranking of a nation to 'improve' as a result of higher ranked nations becoming more dominant.

When analysing position in the medal table on a time series basis it can be difficult to assess actual performance between one Olympiad and another. For example, in Sydney 2000 Great Britain achieved 10th place by virtue of winning 11 gold medals. In Athens 2004 Great Britain also achieved 10th place but on this occasion by winning 9 gold medals. If position in the medal table was the only measure of performance, then 10th place in two consecutive Olympic Games would be said to have been an identical performance. As will be shown later in this chapter when using alternative measures of performance, Great Britain's success in 2000 and 2004 was not identical. The second key weakness with the medal table is that it ignores the totality of achievement in much the same way that assessing capital investment projects using the payback method ignores the life time of a project. To illustrate this point a second excerpt from the Athens 2004 medal table is reproduced in Table 4.4.

Table 4.4: Excerpt from Athens 2004 medal table (b)

Nation	Gold	Silver	Bronze	Medals
2. People's Republic of China CHN	32	17	14	63
3. Russian Federation RUS	27	27	38	92

In the Athens medal table China was ranked above Russia as a result of having won 32 gold medals compared with Russia's 27 gold medals. However, this ranking ignores the fact that Russia won 92 medals overall compared with China's 63.

Various methods have been used to re-analyse the Olympic medal tables to allow for the totality of achievement. The most basic of these is to list nations according to the total number of medals won. Using this method on Tables 4.3 and 4.4 would place Russia ahead of China. The total medals system can also be used to a limited extent on time series data. Figure 4.9 below illustrates the performance of Great Britain in the Summer Olympic Games 1948 - 2004.

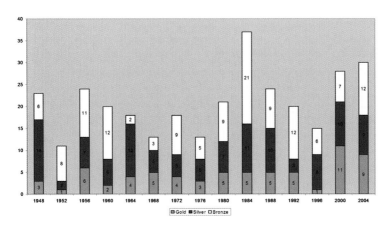

Figure 4.9: Great Britain in the Summer Olympic Games 1948 - 2004 - Total Medals

If we ignore the boycotted Olympics between 1976 and 1984, there has been only one instance in which the number of medals won by Great Britain has increased in two consecutive editions of the Olympic Games, i.e. 1996 - 2004. This period follows the introduction of the World Class Performance Programme in 1997. In short, Great Britain has never won more medals in non-boycotted Olympic Games than it has since the introduction of the World Class Performance Programme. A similar situation is true for the Netherlands following the creation of NOC*NSF in 1993 and subsequent investment in elite sport as shown in Figure 4.10.

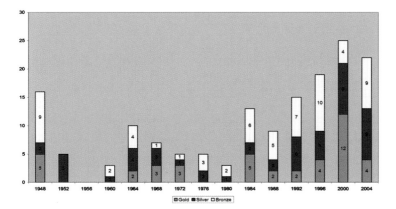

Figure 4.10:
The Netherlands
in the Summer
Olympic Games
1948 - 2004 -
Total Medals

However, even the total medals system itself is limited because it does not take into account the relative value of medals. Taken to its logical conclusion one gold medal under the total medals system would be equal to one silver medal or one bronze medal. Thus in Figure 4.9 if the total medals method is adopted, Great Britain's performance appears to have been better in 2004 (30 medals) than 2000 (28 medals). There is a strong argument to suggest that the 'quality' of medals won in 2000 (more gold, more silver and less bronze) was higher than in 2004. For this reason, we discount total medals as a measure of performance in favour of a system that discriminates between the quality of medals won.

A method which allows for the relative values of gold, silver and bronze medals is a 'points' system which recognises the relative value of medals and makes use of a weighting system to convert a nation's medal haul into a points equivalent. The most simple points system is to award 3 points for a gold medal, 2 for a silver medal and 1 for a bronze medal. Applying this points system to the Athens 2004 medal table would elevate Russia to 2nd position (173 points) at the expense of China (144 points) who would slip to third place. A modified version of Table 4.4 to illustrate the point is repeated below.

Table 4.5 (4.4 Modified): Excerpt from Athens 2004 medal table (b)

Nation	Gold	Silver	Bronze	Medals	Points
2. Russian Federation RUS	27	27	38	92	173
3. People's Republic of China CHN	32	17	14	63	144

[China points = ((32*3)+(17*2)+(14*1)) = 144]

The advantage of the points system is that it converts relative performance to absolute performance and takes into account the totality of achievement. Therefore, it is a more useful measure of the performance of an elite athlete production system for strategic planning and decision making purposes than the official Olympic Games' medal table. Applying the points system described above to the cases of Great Britain, the Netherlands and Belgium gives the time series analysis shown in Figure 4.11.

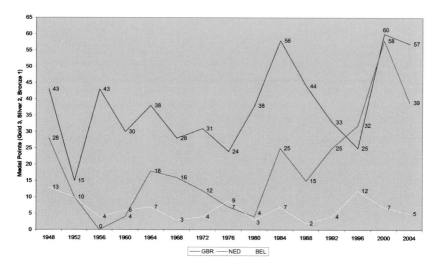

Figure 4.11: Sample nations in the Summer Olympic Games 1948 - 2004 - Total Points

For GBR Figure 4.11 shows a random pattern of performance between 1948 and 1976; growth during the boycotted Games of 1980 and 1984; a period of constant decline between 1984 and 1996 and then considerable recovery and stabilisation in 2000 and 2004. It is worth noting that the points system confirms Sydney 2000 (60 points) was a greater level of achievement than Athens 2004 (57 points) because the points value of the medals won in Sydney was higher. For the Netherlands there was a period of consistent decline from 1960 to 1980, recovery in 1984, decline in 1988 and then four editions of continuous improvement until a reversal in 2004. For Belgium there is no discernible pattern of performance other than random fluctuations between a low of 0, a high of 13, and an average of 6 medal points.

Whilst the points system is a more useful measure of performance than position in the medal table or total medals won, it has one major limitation. As the number of events contested at each Games has varied considerably over time (Figure 4.5) and to a lesser extent the number of points per event has also varied (for example two or more nations 'tieing' for the same medal), the number of points available at each Olympic Games has also varied.

In order to convert points won into a standardised measure, it is necessary to compute 'market share', that is, points won as a proportion of points available to win. Using market share it is possible to make a more accurate diagnosis as to whether the 58 points won in 1984, the 60 points won in 2000 or the 57 points won in 2004 was the best performance by GBR in standardised terms. The results of this analysis are shown in Table 4.6.

Table 4.6: Great Britain's standardised performance using market share

Edition	Gold	Silver	Bronze	Medals	Points	Points Available	Market Share %
1984	5	11	21	37	58	1,359	4.27%
2000	11	10	7	28	60	1,829	3.28%
2004	9	9	12	30	57	1,832	3.11%

An illustration of how the 'market share' indicator works in practice can be seen in a re-analysis of Great Britain's performance in 1984, 2000 and 2004. In the 300 events contested in Sydney a total of 1,829 points was awarded, of which Great Britain and Northern Ireland won 60. This is a market share of 3.28%, which in turn is slightly better than the 57 points won out of 1,832 (301 events) in Athens 2004, a market share of 3.11%.

However, in the sample of the 3 Olympic Games examined in Table 4.6, the performance in Los Angeles is the best performance because the 58 points won from 221 events (1,359 points) gives a market share score of 4.27%. It can therefore be concluded that on a standardised basis, the performance of Great Britain in Sydney 2000 was better than the performance achieved in Athens 2004. Market share for the three SPLISS project partner nations from 1948 to 2004 is shown in Figure 4.12.

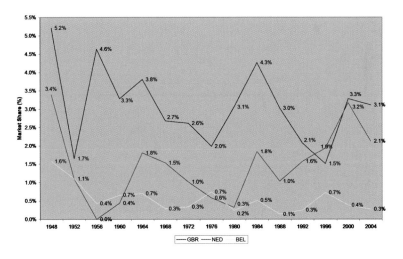

Figure 4.12: SPLISS project partner nations 1948 - 2004 - Market Share

In Figure 4.12 it can be seen that although 2004 was a reversal for the Netherlands after uninterrupted improvement since 1988, the market share achieved in Athens (2.1%) was the Netherlands' third highest score since 1948. By contrast, Sydney 2000 and Athens 2004 represent only the second time in recent history that Belgium's market share has declined in two successive Olympiads (the only other time being 1948 to 1956).

Applying the time series market share analysis to the remaining three nations in the SPLISS project (Italy, Canada and Norway) gives the trend lines shown in Figure 4.13.

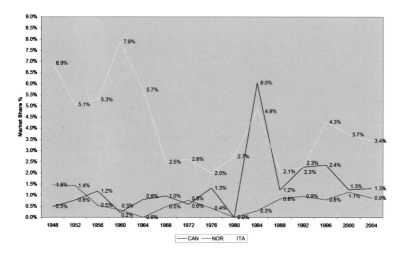

Figure 4.13: SPLISS project other nations 1948 - 2004 - Market Share

Italy is the most consistently successful performing nation shown in Figure 4.13. Its market share peaked at 7.9% in 1960 when the Olympic Games were held in Rome and then declined to a low of 2.0% in Montreal (1976). Increases in performance occurred during the boycotted Olympics of 1980 and 1984 followed by a sharp fall in Seoul 1988. Since 1988 Italy scored a peak market share of 4.4% in Atlanta 1996 and has been on a seemingly gentle downward trend since then to 3.4% in 2004. A better description of Italy's performance since 1996 might be 'relative stability' given the nature of increasing competition for medals discussed earlier. Furthermore, this 'decline' has been sufficient for Italy to perform better than the United Kingdom since 1996.

Between 1948 and 1980 Canada achieved a market share in excess of 1% on just two occasions, 1956 and again in 1976 when it was the host nation. Following a spectacularly successful Olympic Games in 1984 when a market share of 6% was achieved, Canada's performance has stabilised within a range of 1.2% to 2.4%. In the last two summer Olympic Games, Canada's performance has been towards the bottom of the range at 1.3%, which in turn is better than or equal to all of Canada's performances between 1948 and 1980.

In standardised terms, Norway's best performances in the summer Olympic Games were in 1948 and 1952 when market share scores of 1.5% and 1.4% respectively were achieved. The period 1956 to 1984 was one of decline, including 0% market share in 1964; mild recovery to 0.8% in 1972; and consistent decline to 0.3% in 1984. Since 1988 Norway has achieved both improvement and consistency within a band ranging from 0.8% to 1.1% in the last five summer Olympic Games.

When looking at recent performance in the Olympic Games there is a logic to starting with Seoul in 1988 as this was the first games since 1972 that had not been contaminated by some form of boycott. In Figure 4.14 we present the market share performance of all six sample nations from 1988 to 2004.

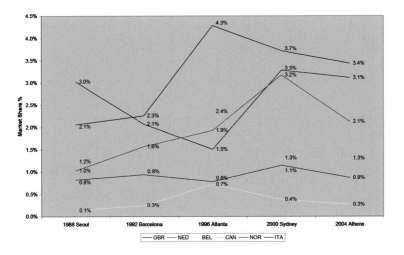

Figure 4.14: SPLISS project all sample nations 1988-2004 – Market Share.

A useful way of contextualising Figure 4.14 is to examine the relative ranking of each nation within the sample on a time series basis, this is shown in Table 4.7.

Table 4.7: Relative rankings of sample nations 1988 - 2004

Nation	1988	1992	1996	2000	2004
United Kingdom	1st	3rd	4th	2nd	2nd
Italy	2nd	1st	1st	1st	1st
Canada	3rd	1st	2nd	4th	4th
Netherlands	4th	4th	3rd	3rd	3rd
Belgium	6th	6th	6th	6th	6th
Norway	5th	5th	5th	5th	5th

Great Britain and Northern Ireland started the time series in first place, fell to fourth in 1996 and has subsequently recovered to second place in 2000 and 2004. Italy has shown great stability being ranked first in every edition except 1988 when it was second. Canada started in third place, improved to joint first place in 1992 and has fallen to fourth place in 2000 and 2004. The Netherlands started in fourth place and showed improvement not just in market share but also in relative ranking to achieve third place in 1996 – a level it has maintained in both 2000 and 2004. Norway and Belgium have been ranked fifth and sixth respectively without fluctuation throughout the time series.

A key question arising from the data presented in Figure 4.14 and Table 4.7, is how might the sample nations be expected to perform given the resources at their disposal? One clear finding emerging from regression analysis is that the two variables which best predict performance in the Summer Olympic Games are population and economic wealth (De Bosscher, De Knop & Heyndels, 2003 a & b). To illustrate the basic point we attempt to answer the question 'how might the sample nations be expected to perform?' by looking at the population and GDP data (Gross Domestic Product, adjusted for Purchasing-Power Parity) for each nation in the context of their performance in Athens 2004 as shown in Table 4.8.

Table 4.8: Resources available to the sample nations and performance diagnosis

Nation	Population	GDP € bn	Athens 2004 Performance Diagnosis	GDP / Head €
United Kingdom	60.4	1,377	Below Expectation	22,880
Italy	58.1	1,281	Above Expectation	22,054
Canada	32.8	792	Below Expectation	24,614
Netherlands	16.4	381	Above Expectation	23,624
Belgium	10.4	247	Below Expectation	24,036
Norway	4.6	141	Above Expectation	31,222

[Source: http://www.cia.gov/cia/publications/factbook/ (2004)- currency modified from $US to € using a currency conversion of 1€ = 1.21$ US]

In Table 4.8 there is a high correlation between population and total GDP for all six sample nations. For example the United Kingdom has the highest population and the highest GDP. Conversely, Norway has the lowest population and the lowest GDP. If actual performance was determined by population and GDP it would be expected that the United Kingdom would be the best performing nation in the sample. In practice, using market share as the most robust measure of performance, Table 4.8 when linked to Table 4.7, reveals that Italy was the best performing nation in Athens 2004 and that this performance was above what might realistically be expected from the nation that was ranked second in both population and GDP. It might therefore be argued that Italy had been more efficient in its use of resources than Great Britain and Northern Ireland as it had out performed a 'wealthier' nation.

In the middle of the distribution in Table 4.8 Canada is diagnosed as having performed below expectation. Given that Canada has a population precisely twice that of the Netherlands and a highly comparable GDP per head, it would be reasonable to expect that Canada would out perform the Netherlands. The fact that this was not the case, indicates that the Netherlands was more efficient at using its resources to achieve success than Canada in Athens 2004.

Similarly at the tail of the distribution, Belgium (10.4m) has a population that is greater than that of Norway (4.6) by a factor of 2.26. Thus it would be reasonable to expect Belgium to out perform Norway in Athens 2004. Again, the fact that this was not the case, indicates that Norway was more efficient at using its resources to achieve success than Belgium in Athens 2004. Consequently, it can be argued that Norway performed above expectation and Belgium performed below expectation.

Market share analysis can also be used to compare standardised performance by gender. Men and women contest a different number of events in the Olympic Games and thus to compare how a nation's male athletes perform relative to their female counterparts, the computation of market share by gender provides a standardised basis from which to make an objective assessment. This type of analysis confirms that in the case of Great Britain, men consistently outperform women in standardised terms, whereas for the Netherlands the reverse is true. Furthermore, market share analysis can be applied at individual sport level as an indicator of the effect of given performance programmes and the systems responsible for delivering them. In the case of the Netherlands, the nation has enjoyed considerable recent success in swimming in the Olympic Games and World Championships as shown by the trend lines in Figure 4.15.

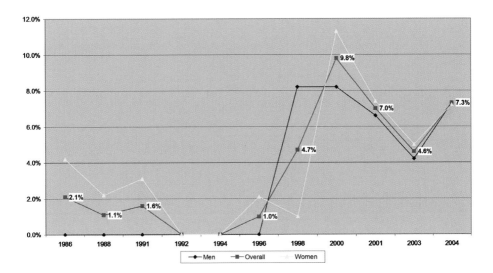

Figure 4.15: Market share for the Netherlands

In Figure 4.15 it can be seen that between 1986 and 1996 all of the Netherlands' success in swimming was attributable to women swimmers. The World Swimming Championships of 1998 heralded a new era in elite swimming with the emergence of Pieter van den Hoogenband. This success was built upon in the Sydney Olympic Games in 2000 when van den Hoogenband and Inge de Bruijn won five gold medals between them.

Although not quite as successful in Athens 2004 as Sydney 2000, it can still be seen that there has been a sustained increase in performance by swimmers representing the Netherlands from 1996 to 2004 compared with performance from 1986 to 1996. In addition, Figure 4.15 confirms that the Netherlands' best performance in standardised terms was at the Sydney Olympics in 2000 when it achieved a market share of 9.8% – its highest market share in all world and Olympic swimming events during the period 1986 to 2004.

The limitation of the portfolio of analysis techniques reviewed thus far is that it is possible that conflicting messages can be given about performance. This point is perhaps best illustrated by examining the case of Great Britain in the two most recent summer Olympic Games. A full breakdown of performance using four different measures is shown in Table 4.9.

Table 4.9: Conflicting measures of performance

Method	2000	2004	Performance
Position in medal table	10th	10th	Same
Total medals	28	30	Better
Points	60	57	Worse
Market share %	3.28%	3.11%	Worse

Depending on the performance measure adopted, Table 4.9 illustrates that it is possible for perfectly reasonable arguments to be made that Great Britain's performance has remained the same, improved or deteriorated. This is hardly a satisfactory position for UK Sport to be in when trying to justify an investment of £84m on support for elite athlete development during the Athens Olympiad. However, of the four measures outlined in Table 4.9 it is our view that market share is the best indicator of a nation's performance.

The justification of this view is twofold. First, market share is the only standardised measure of the four performance indicators shown in Table 4.9. Second, market share can be increased in one of three ways:

- an increase in the number of medals won;
- an increase in the quality of medals won; or
- maintaining absolute performance when the number of events has declined.

These are much more robust and controllable measures of success than moving up the medal table simply because superior nations have become even more dominant or close rivals have deteriorated. The basic point about the value of market share as a measure holds true whether we are examining an aggregate of sports, as in the Olympic Games, or an individual sport in isolation.

It is not only the performance of the United Kingdom that fluctuates according to the type of measure used. For the remaining five nations in the sample we have replicated the analysis shown in Table 4.9. A full breakdown of the change in performance by measurement type is shown in Table 4.10.

Table 4.10: Change in performance 2000 - 2004 by measure type

Nation	Medal Table Position	Total Medals	Points (3,2,1)	Market Share %
United Kingdom	Same	Better	Worse	Worse
Canada	Better	Worse	Better	Better
Italy	Worse	Worse	Worse	Worse
Norway	Better	Worse	Worse	Worse
The Netherlands	Worse	Worse	Worse	Worse
Belgium	Better	Worse	Worse	Worse

With the exception of Italy and the Netherlands, who both performed worse according to every measure in Table 4.10, there are differing diagnoses for the remaining nations depending on the measure selected. Canada performed better on three of the four measures and was the only nation to have increased its market share. As Canada experienced a decrease in the total number of medals won, it follows that market share must have been increased by an improvement in the quality of the medals won. This point is proven by the fact Canada's performance in 2004 was 3 gold, 6 silver and 3 bronze (24 points) medals compared with 3 gold, 3 silver and 8 bronze medals in 2000 (23 points). By contrast, Belgium improved its ranking in the medal table by winning a gold medal in 2004, thereby ranking it ahead of all other nations that won any medal other than a gold medal. By every other measure used in Table 4.10, Belgium's performance in 2004 was worse than in 2000.

The analysis thus far has focused on performance in the summer Olympic Games, which although a truly global event, is not a measure of success in all sports. To illustrate the point, the winter Olympic Games, which are particularly important to Nordic and Alpine nations, are not included in the preceding analysis. Later in the report (section 4.7) we address this point with some analysis devoted entirely to performance in the winter Olympic Games. Furthermore, the Olympic medal table is but a snapshot of global sporting prowess at a given point in time and does not necessarily represent global sporting achievement for the duration of each Olympiad. Some 28 sports and 35 disciplines are contested at the Olympic Games and in the UK over 100 sports are formally recognised by the national agencies of sport. Therefore, the Olympics are but a subset of all sports and inevitably for some nations culturally important sports do not figure in the Olympic programme, for example rugby and cricket in the case of 'Commonwealth' nations.

In some sports, success in the Olympic Games is not recognised as the pinnacle of achievement, notably tennis where Grand Slam tournaments are widely regarded as being the pinnacle of achievement; and in football the FIFA World Cup. Therefore for nations which view themselves as 'sporting' nations there needs to be another measure to contextualise overall sporting achievement. This measure needs to be able to change more frequently than once every four years and also needs to rate recent success more highly than historical success. A model to deliver these requirements has been devised by UK Sport called the World Sporting Index and it is discussed in Section 4.5.

4.5   Developing market share
– the world sporting index

UK Sport has developed a World Sporting Index to derive a continuous, regularly updatable measure of success in a portfolio of 60 different sports. In essence the World Sporting Index is an adaptation of market share, as discussed in Section 4, and the system is used in two ways: first, to compute market share in individual sports; and, second to derive an overall sporting index for a portfolio of 60 sports.

In individual sports, points are awarded to the top 8 places where a gold medal is worth 10 points, silver 8, bronze 6 and 8th place 1 point. For every event where there are 8 finalists there are 39 points, which when multiplied by the number of events, gives total points available from which market share calculations can be computed. It is possible to weight different events according to their perceived importance, for example in athletics the World Indoor Championships might be weighted 1, the World Outdoor Championships 2, and the Olympic Games 3.

A test of reasonableness of the UK Sport World Sporting Index applied to tennis can be gauged by assessing performance in the 2004 Olympics (weighted 1), the 2004 Davis / Federation Cups (weighted 2) and the 2004 Grand Slam events (weighted 3). The top 10 nations are listed below in Table 4.11.

Table 4.11: UK Sport Sporting Index applied to tennis

Rank	Nation	Market share (%)
1	USA	19.0
2	Russia	17.1
3	Argentina	10.1
4	Switzerland	9.0
5	France	8.6
6	Belgium	5.6
7	Spain	5.3
8	Australia	3.9
9	UK	3.3
10	Croatia	2.4

Whilst there may be disagreement over the precise ordering of some of the nations listed in Table 4.11, most people with an interest in tennis would concur that the list of nations accurately reflects the balance of power in world tennis in 2004. This would therefore suggest that the Sporting Index is a reasonable measure of performance in the sport of tennis.

The same technique outlined above for tennis is also applied by UK Sport to 60 major sports in order to derive a World Sporting Index. For the sake of simplicity, the points awarded for 1st, 2nd and 3rd only are used to produce the World Sporting Index. The scores for the portfolio of 60 sports are computed to give a market share score which in turn can be weighted in one of three ways: first, on the basis of treating all sports as equals (no weighting); second, on the basis of public preferences (sports in which the UK public would like to have success are weighted the highest, e.g. football); and, third, Olympic sports are weighted on the basis of UK Sport's strategic priorities. At the end of 2004 (i.e. following the Athens Olympics), the top ten nations in the World Sporting Index plus the Netherlands and Belgium were as listed below in Table 4.12.

Table 4.12: The top 10 nations in the World Index 2004

Rank	Nation	Market share (%)
1	USA	11.2
2	Germany	8.1
3	Australia	7.5
4	Russia	7.1
5	United Kingdom	6.5
6	France	5.3
7	China	5.1
8	New Zealand	4.0
9	Italy	3.7
10	Canada	3.2
11	Norway	2.7
18	Netherlands	1.6
37	Belgium	0.4

As a test of reasonableness, the top seven nations in the list above all finished in the top ten of the final Athens 2004 Olympic medal table. Canada makes the list primarily because of its success in Winter sports; and New Zealand makes the list mainly for its prowess in team sports. As in the case of tennis discussed above (Table 4.11), most people with an interest in sport would concur that the list of ten nations above is a reasonable assessment of the balance of power in world sport. Between December 2003 and December 2004, the following top ten nations, in ranked order, all increased their market share: Italy, UK, NZ, Japan, France, Germany and China. The USA, though starting from a high base, saw its market share fall by the greatest amount, followed by Australia, Canada and Russia.

As World Sporting Index results are compiled on the basis of all eligible events within a four year Olympic cycle, consideration is now being given to down weighting the value of points by 25% per year so that recent performance is worth more than past performance. This possible development reflects the desire to make the model a more comprehensive measure of performance than simply medals won. The model already makes a distinction between the 'quality' of events: in future it may also incorporate an element of 'the time value of success'. The UK Sport World Sporting Index can be used for time series analysis so that performance over the period of an Olympiad can be assessed. To illustrate the point, Table 4.13 below shows the changes in points won and market share for the six sample nations.

Table 4.13: The sample nations 2000 - 2004

Nation	2000 Points	2000 Market Share	2004 Points	2004 Market Share	Change in Market Share[1]
United Kingdom	431	7.2%	387	6.5%	-11%
Canada	211	3.5%	220	3.2%	-9%
Italy	189	3.1%	191	3.2%	3%
Norway	167	2.8%	163	2.7%	-4%
Netherlands	123	2.1%	95	1.6%	-31%
Belgium	15	0.3%	22	0.4%	25%

1 [Change in Market Share = ((2004 MS - 2000 MS) / (2000 MS)) * 100]

As discussed in the context of Tables 4.9 and 4.10, an increase in market share is arguably the most robust and controllable measure of overall performance. If this point is accepted it can be seen from Table 4.13 that Belgium (25%) and Italy (3%) increased their market share between 2000 and 2004; whereas the United Kingdom (-11%), the Netherlands (-31%), Canada (-9%) and Norway (-4%) have all experienced a reduction in market share. The performance of Belgium (+25%) over the four year period is largely attributable to the success of tennis players Kim Clijsters and Justine Henin. The decline of the Netherlands (-31%) is largely attributable to a relatively poor Olympic Games in 2004 compared with 2002 (4 gold medals vs. 12 gold medals). However, it should be noted that in 2004 even after a decline relative to 2000, the Netherlands achieves four times the market share of Belgium with less than double the population of Belgium and 25% of the UK's market with a population that is 27% of the UK population.

In short, the application of market share analysis modified for the importance of a given event, down weighted by time factors, and up weighted by public perception or strategic priority, can give a reasonable indication of performance in a single sport or a portfolio of numerous sports. In the absence of any globally recognised measures of all round performance in sport, the UK Sport World Sporting Index is a useful barometer of the broad balance of power within world sport. Inevitably there will be suggestions that the weighting systems introduce a degree of subjectivity to the process. Nonetheless, the results produced thus far by the system are credible and would pass any test of 'reasonableness'.

A useful feature of the UK Sport World Sporting Index is that the portfolio of 60 sports can be analysed in a variety of ways so that a more focused perspective on performance can be taken. This flexibility of analysis is particularly helpful for nations which might prioritise winter Olympic sports over summer Olympic sports, or Olympic sports generally over non-Olympic sports. To illustrate how the rankings of nations can change according to the nature of sports included within the analysis, Table 4.14 has been constructed to illustrate four potential uses of the UK Sport World Sporting Index. The first column repeats the data from Table 4.12 to show broad sporting performance over 60 sports; the second column shows performance over Olympic sports only (summer and winter combined); the third column shows performance in the summer Olympic Games only; and the fourth column shows performance in the winter Olympic Games only.

Table 4.14: The relative performance of the sample nations by index type

Nation	All 60 Sports	All Olympic Sports	Summer Olympic Sports	Winter Olympic Sports
United Kingdom	6.5% (1st)	2.2% (4th)	2.5% (2nd)	2.1% (5th)
Canada	3.2% (2nd)	4.0% (1st)	0.8% (4th)	13.2% (1st)
Italy	3.2% (3rd)	3.8% (2nd)	4.3% (1st)	3.0% (3rd)
Norway	2.7% (4th)	2.6% (3rd)	0.6% (5th)	9.9% (2nd)
Netherlands	1.6% (5th)	1.9% (5th)	2.1% (3rd)	2.1% (4th)
Belgium	0.4% (6th)	0.3% (6th)	0.5% (6th)	0.0% (6th)

From Table 4.14 it can be seen that with the exception of Belgium, which is consistently ranked 6th out of 6, the rankings of the other sample nations vary markedly by index type. It is our view that this type of variation gives an important insight into the broad sporting priorities of each nation. Some nations seem to have policies which are 'diversity' based and others seem to favour a more focused or 'priority' based approach.

The UK is a good example of a seemingly diversity oriented nation. It is ranked 1st in the index of 60 sports but only 4th in the index of all Olympic sports. This finding can in part be explained by a high ranking for summer Olympic sports (2nd) and a low ranking (5th) for winter Olympic sports. This enables us to diagnose that the UK's success in world sport is driven primarily by a focus on summer Olympic sports and non-Olympic sports.

By contrast, Canada is ranked 2nd in the 60 sport index largely because if its dominance in winter Olympic sports which is so strong that it is capable of ranking Canada 1st in all Olympic sports, despite only achieving a ranking of 4th in the summer Olympic sports index. Italy is ranked 3rd in the 60 sport index and this is primarily because of its 1st place ranking in the summer Olympic sport index. Closer inspection of Italy's performance suggests that it is a nation that performs well in all Olympic sports as it is rated 2nd in this index but only 3rd in the 60 sport index. Finally, Norway mirrors Canada on a smaller scale. Its high winter Olympic sport index (2nd) is sufficient to place it 3rd in the all Olympic sport index, despite being ranked only 5th in the summer Olympic sport index and 4th in the 60 sport index.

For research purposes, the key point arising from Table 4.14 is that it is problematic to compare nations' performance as priorities in each nation may be different. There is little to be gained by using the 60 sport index to compare one nation against another when for example the UK might support 28 of these sports and Norway only 12. It would be equally problematic to agree identical common ground between two nations when measuring sporting performance as social and cultural factors are likely to ensure that no two nations have identical priorities. Similarly the problem of comparing policies is compounded by the likelihood that national policies in one nation are likely to be focused on a different portfolio of priorities than potential comparator nations. There is little point in trying to make meaningful comparison between Canada or Norway and the UK as the former nations support winter Olympic sports and the latter supports a much broader range of sports and explicitly does not prioritise winter Olympic sports. The net effect of this finding is that we suggest purer comparisons will be made in the future if the analysis focuses on specific sports rather than portfolios of sports.

CHAPTER 4

During the research programme it was discovered that in Canada a similar system to the UK Sport World Sporting Index had been developed and was in regular use by Sport Canada. To test the comparability of the UK and Canada systems, and therefore implicitly their 'reasonableness', we present in Table 4.15 a comparison of the absolute and relative rankings of the sample nations. Both systems use an aggregate ranking for sports and disciplines conducted in both the summer and winter Olympic Games. The basic principles of the two systems are similar, that is market share, but the method in which scores are allocated and weighted is unique to each system.

Table 4.15: UK Sport Sporting Index v Canadian Equivalent

Nation	UK Sport Absolute	UK Sport Relative	Sport Canada Absolute	Sport Canada Relative
United Kingdom	14th	4th	12th	4th
Canada	6th	1st	8th	2nd
Italy	7th	2nd	7th	1st
Norway	13th	3rd	9th	3rd
Netherlands	17th	5th	13th	5th
Belgium	42nd	6th	Not Ranked	6th

The only difference between the UK Sport and the Sport Canada rankings is that in the former Canada is first and Italy second, whereas in the latter Italy is first and Canada second. All other relative rankings are identical. The consistency between the two systems suggests that there is a degree of reliability between them. Furthermore it may be possible to develop a genuine world sporting index that embraces the diversity of sports played whilst achieving wider acceptance of the underlying principles. The flexibility of databases means that it is possible to sub analyse any index of sporting performance into an agreed portfolio that facilitates meaningful transnational comparison. Similarly, in the event of a portfolio of sports being inappropriate, comparisons can be made on a sport by sport basis.

4.6 Regression analysis

The relationship between sporting success, as defined by points scored in the UK Sport Sporting Index (or indeed other rankings such as medal tables), and most macro-variables that are indicated as important in a range of literature (population, wealth, religion, area, degree of urbanization) can be tested statistically using regression analysis (Ordinary Least Squares (OLS) regression). This methodology was adopted from De Bosscher, De Knop and Heyndels (2003 a & b) as a way to measure 'relative' success of nations controlling for macro variables. The authors analyse the residuals as an indicator of efficient elite sport policies of nations. When the regression analysis is applied to the UK Sport World Sporting Index, the net result is that population (34%) and GDP per capita (17%) 'explain' on average 51% of a nation's sporting success.

Perhaps of most relevance for this research, the regression analysis enables us to predict a nation's sporting success (dependent variable) using the independent variables of population and GPD per capita. Furthermore, by comparing a nation's actual score with its predicted score, it is possible to assess whether the nation concerned has performed above, below or equal to expectation.

The results from the regression analysis for the six sample nations are outlined in Table 4.16.

Table 4.16: Results of the regression analysis base on population and GDP / capita

Nation	Overall Rank	Residual[1]	Diagnosis	Sample Rank
Italy	5th	79.1	Better than predicted	1st
United Kingdom	18th	16.2	Better than predicted	2nd
Netherlands	24th	10.8	Better than predicted	3rd
Canada	64th	-35.1	Worse than predicted	4th
Norway	72nd	-62.0	Worse than predicted	5th
Belgium	68th	-41.5	Worse than predicted	6th

[1]Residual = variation that cannot be explained by the macro level variables

The sample rank of the SPLISS consortium in Table 4.16 is identical to that shown for the six nations in the Olympic Games of both 2000 and 2004 (Table 4.7). However, of greater interest is the finding that the United Kingdom, Italy and the Netherlands all performed better than the regression model predicted, whereas Canada, Belgium and Norway all performed worse. Italy is the best performing nation in the sample and also has the highest residual value. This in turn means that not only did Italy perform better than predicted, it also performed better in standardised terms than the United Kingdom and the Netherlands which have lower residual scores of 16.2 and 10.8 respectively. Similarly, Norway performed worse than predicted (residual -62.0) and this performance was worse in standardised terms than Canada (residual -35.1) and Belgium (residual -41.5) by virtue of Norway having the highest negative residual of these three nations. Norway is 'penalised' in the regression as a result of having the highest GDP per capita of the sample nations (see Table 4.8).

For the better performing nations, it can be concluded that they have achieved greater sporting success than their population and GDP per capita values alone would predict. This conclusion then helps to form the subsequent research question, that is, 'how much of this better than expected performance is as a result of the nations concerned taking a successful strategic approach to the development of elite athletes and their supporting infrastructure?' Similarly, for the nations' performing worse than predicted, the subsequent research questions are 'given these nations resources, why are they performing worse than might be expected?' and 'how much of this under performance can be attributed to policy factors?' In terms of performance measurement, the regression analysis provides us with the basis for yet another way in which to assess the relative performance of the sample nations.

4.7   The Winter Olympic Games

The preceding analysis has focused primarily on the Summer Olympic Games and a portfolio of 60 sports included in the UK Sport World Sporting Index. Whilst the World Sporting Index does include Winter Olympic disciplines, their significance is diluted amongst the 35 disciplines of the Summer Olympic Games and the other non-Olympic sports which comprise the 60 sport World Sporting Index. Thus there is the danger that nations which particularly value success in the Winter Olympic Games, notably Nordic and Alpine nations in Europe, should be able to apply the same analysis as that presented earlier in this chapter. To this end we have replicated Figure 4.14 and Table 4.7 for the last five editions of the Winter Olympic Games and these are shown in Figure 4.16 and Table 4.17 respectively.

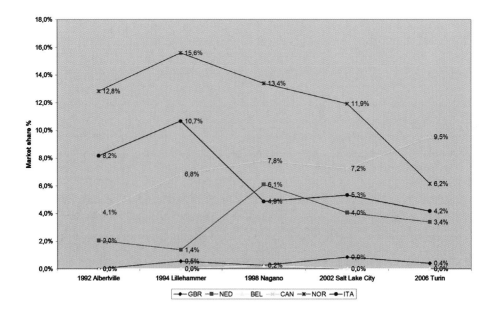

Figure 4.16: SPLISS sample nations market share in Winter Olympics 1992-2006

As per the previous analysis, a useful way of contextualising Figure 4.16 is by examining the relative ranking of each nation within the sample on a time series basis as shown in Table 4.17.

Table 4.17: Relative rankings of sample nations 1992-2006

Nation	1992	1994	1998	2002	2006
Norway	1st	1st	1st	1st	3rd
Italy	2nd	2nd	4th	3rd	2nd
Canada	3rd	3rd	2nd	2nd	1st
Netherlands	4th	4th	3rd	4th	4th
United Kingdom	Not ranked	5th	5th	5th	5th
Belgium	Not ranked	Not ranked	5th	Not ranked	Not ranked

Figure 4.16 and Table 4.17 show a greater volatility in overall performance than the equivalent for the Summer Olympic Games. Norway begins the time series in first place, a position which they maintain, despite falling market share, until 2006 when it falls to second place. Italy starts in second place and achieves a highest market share of 10.7% in 1994 before falling to fourth place in 1994 and third place in 2002, in both instances less than half the market share (4.9% and 5.3% respectively) achieved in 1994. In Torino 2006 it maintains its position with a slight decrease in market share (4.2%) despite the fact that Italy was the host nation.

Canada is the best performing nation in the sample as a result of improving its ranking and market share in 1992 from third and 4.1% respectively, to first place with a market share of 9.5% in 2006. Canada will host the 2010 Winter Olympic Games and has the publicly stated aim of topping the medal table at Vancouver. In order to meet this aim, and judging by the performance of Canadian athletes in contemporary editions of the winter Olympic Games, it would appear that there has been considerable prioritisation of and investment in elite level Winter Olympic sports in Canada.

The Netherlands is consistently placed fourth in the time series apart from 1998 when it had its best Winter Olympics in recent years and Italy had its worst year in the time series. The United Kingdom is consistently placed fifth in the time series apart from 1992 when Team GB did not win a medal. Belgium has won a medal at only one of the last five Winter Olympics and thus is not ranked in four out five editions and achieves joint fifth place in 1998.

Whilst the key purpose of this chapter has been to quantify the performance of the sample nations, a secondary aim has been to demonstrate a methodology by which an objective assessment of performance can be made using techniques that are easily understood by the sport policy community. This section has shown that the evaluation framework is equally applicable to the winter Olympic Games and that the performance of the sample nations in the Winter Olympics is significantly different to their performance in the Summer Olympics and the UK Sport World Sporting Index.

4.8   Alternative measures of performance

Whilst medal based measures of performance are easily understood measures of success, they still ignore the totality of achievement of an elite sport programme. As has already been demonstrated competition for medals is increasing as more nations take part in the Olympic Games (Figure 4.7). It is quite possible for Performance Directors in individual sports to make considerable progress in developing a sport without this progress being recognised by medals in elite competition. Some of these alternative measures of success are outlined below.

The number of athletes qualifying to take part in elite championships
The global nature of the Olympic Games is such that for some nations and individual sports the number of athletes who qualify to contest an event at the Games is a valid measure of performance. In Athens 2004 only one boxer qualified to represent Great Britain in a tournament in which it was possible to qualify eleven boxers. A successful output from the Amateur Boxing Association's elite athlete programme for 2008 might be the qualification of 2 or more boxers to take part in the event – regardless of their ultimate performance. Taken to a strategic level, the number of events a nation qualifies to contest could be taken as a valid measure of performance for any nation. In 2004, 301 events were contested in Ahens and a valid measure of performance for a national sports federation might be the number, or proportion, of events that the nation concerned qualified to take part in. Similarly, although there are 301 events it does not follow that each nation can contest every medal. Whilst it is possible for USA to win gold, silver and bronze in the 100m in athletics, the eight nations contesting the softball tournament can win only one medal. Thus yet another measure of performance might be the number of medals contested. In Athens 2004 the maximum number of medals that any nation could contest was 486, which in turn was less than half of the total medals awarded.

The number of athletes qualifying to contest the final of an event
In high profile sports such as swimming or athletics, in which finals are often contested by 8 (and sometimes more) athletes, simply qualifying for the final may well be a considerable achievement. This point is particularly true for smaller nations which have fewer athletes and resources to draw upon than larger more affluent nations. As an example, it might be more of an achievement for a Belgian sprinter to reach the final of the men's athletics 100m final than for an athlete representing the USA to win the bronze medal. The threshold of performance can be lowered to recognise achievement in any of the various rounds between basic qualifying and the final. For example, it would be a great achievement for a sprinter from the Cayman Islands to qualify for the Olympic Games and to proceed beyond the first round. It is this more comprehensive view of 'performance' that will help with the broad aim of this project to identify over and under achieving nations in a systematic manner.

The number of athletes posting 'seasonal' best performances
In an environment of increasing competition globally, the best that might reasonably be expected of an athlete would be for them to achieve a season's best performance in their event. This type of measure can be used as a good indicator of Performance Directors delivering athletes in peak condition for a major championship.

The number of athletes achieving personal bests or breaking national records
As a logical extension of seasonal best times being a valid measure of performance, it follows that more demanding measures such as lifetime (personal) best performances and all time national best performances are also valid measures of performance. It is less easy to be critical about an athlete who was eliminated in the semi-final of an Olympic final and who in so doing broke a national record. This type of performance indicates positive 'distance' travelled in terms of the achievement of a given nation whilst at the same time acknowledging that standards have improved globally. Thus the narrowing of the gap between a national record and the level of performance required to achieve medal winning success in a major championship is also a valid measure of success.

One of the reasons why interim measures of success such as those listed above are particularly valid is that one of the ingredients of a successful elite sports development programme is time. Australia performed exceptionally well in the Olympic Games in 2000 and 2004 and this success is widely attributed to the establishment of the Australian Institute of Sport in the late 1970s following a poor showing in Montreal 1976. In addition, France has also performed well in the Olympic Games since perceived failure in the 1960 Olympic Games in Rome, the 1975 Mazeaud legislation requiring support of elite athletes, and the establishment of the French National Institute of Sport and Physical Education (INSEP) in 1976.

In Italy there has been a strategic approach to the development of elite sport since 1942 when the Italian National Olympic Committee (CONI) was given the rights to sports-related gambling profits. These monies have been used to support state, regional and local level networks of elite athlete development. A simple measure of the system's success can be appreciated by comparing Italy's performance in the Summer Olympic Games with that of Great Britain, as shown in Figure 4.17.

Figure 4.17: Italy v Great Britain in the Olympic medal table 1948 - 2004

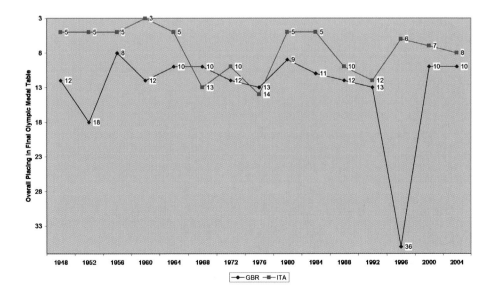

In 15 editions of the Olympic Games between 1948 and 2004 Italy has been ranked ahead of Great Britain on 13/15 occasions. Italy has been investing in elite sports development systems since 1942, whereas in Great Britain the systematic programme of investment did not begin until 1997. France has enjoyed a long term increase in its performance in the Olympic Games since 1976. Since 1980, Great Britain and Northern Ireland has been ranked in the top ten nations in the summer Olympic Games on one occasion (1980). By contrast, in the same period France, which has an identical population to the UK (60m), has been ranked outside the top ten nations on only one occasion (1984). Thus using the examples of Italy and France as earlier investors in a strategic approach to elite sport than the UK, it is reasonable to conclude that time can be considered to be a factor in determining the success of an elite sports development system.

4.9   Measuring the financial efficiency of success

The measures discussed thus far, whether they be the four indicators of success reviewed in Tables 4.9 and 4.10 or the interim measures of success discussed in Section 4.8 are all measures of performance. In a world in which resources are limited, a further measure that should be considered is financial efficiency in terms of examining the amount of resource used to deliver a specified level of performance.

In the UK there was a National Audit Office review of UK Sport's World Class Performance Programme following the Olympic Games of Athens 2004[6]. Part of this review has led to the compilation of a table of inputs (money invested in given sports), outputs (medals won in Athens 2004) and efficiency (cost per medal won). This is the first time that comprehensive analysis of actual performance compared with planned performance in Olympic sport has been made publicly available in the UK. Perhaps of most value to researchers is that the data has been collated in a manner which permits legitimate comparisons across sports. An adapted version of this data is shown in Table 4.18.

At a summary level Table 4.18 shows that the 28 medals won by sports funded by UK Sport cost an average of € 3.54m each. However, as fewer medals were won (28) than had been targeted (39) the actual cost of medals at € 3.54m each was considerably higher than the budgeted cost of € 2.54m. This 'cost over run' was in part driven by six sports failing to win any of the medals they had targeted.

When looking at individual sports the average cost per medal fluctuates from a low of € 440,000 for a medal (bronze) in archery to a high of € 4.75m per medal in swimming (two bronze medals). It is a salutary point to note that the bronze medals in swimming cost eleven times more than their equivalent in archery. It is clear that some medals cost more than others to win and that the average cost per medal is driven up by the high profile sports (in the UK) of swimming, athletics and rowing.

---

6   http://www.nao.org.uk/publications/nao_reports/04-05/0405182.pdf

Table 4.18: Funding and medals won by UK Sport-funded[1] Olympic Sports (2004)

Sport	Funding m	Medal Target	Medals Won	Target Cost per Medal € m	Actual Cost per Medal € m
Swimming	9.49	-	2	-	4.75
Athletics	16.50	7	4	€ 2.36	4.12
Rowing	15.48	3	4	€ 5.16	3.87
Cycling	11.83	5	4	€ 2.37	2.96
Modern Pentathlon	2.92	1	1	€ 2.92	2.92
Canoeing	6.86	2	3	€ 3.43	2.29
Sailing	10.51	3	5	€ 3.50	2.10
Diving	2.04	2	1	€ 1.02	2.04
Equestrian	4.67	2	3	€ 2.34	1.56
Archery	0.44	1	1	€ 0.44	0.44
Gymnastics	6.13	3	0	€ 2.04	
Judo	5.11	2	0	€ 2.56	
Triathlon	3.80	2	0	€ 1.90	
Shooting	2.19	3	0	€ 0.73	
Taekwondo	0.88	2	0	€ 0.44	
Weightlifting	0.15	1	0	€ 0.15	
Total	98.99	39	28	€ 2.54	€ 3.54

[1] Although Great Britain and Northern Ireland won 30 medals in Athens 2004, Table 4.18 contains details of only 28 medals. This is because, through to 2004. boxing and badminton were organised and funded at home nation level rather than UK level.

The Belgian partners in the SPLISS project have compiled similar data to the UK and the key figures for the three sports in which Belgium, (only Flanders) won medals are shown in Table 4.19.

Table 4.19: Table 4.18 applied to Flanders

Sport	Funding € m	Medals Won	Actual Cost per Medal €m
Cycling	€ 1.31	1	0.76
Judo	€ 1.18	1	1.18
Other sports	€ 10.78	0	n/a
Total	€ 13.27	2	6.64

For Flanders, the average cost of medals in those sports which won a medal in Athens 2004 was €1.25m, which was less than the cost of all the UK medals won except in archery. However, this understates the true cost of medals won by athletes from Flanders as it excludes the investment in sports which did not win medals. Allowing for investment which was not successful, the true cost of medals for Flanders was € 6.64m, which was more than € 3m per medal more than for the UK. Currently the research is insufficiently developed to be able to make detailed comparisons between the cost of medals won by nations. We can be confident that the cost per medal calculations reflect the cost of investment of the bodies concerned, that is, UK Sport in the UK and BLOSO in Flanders. What is not clear is the extent to which cost per medal figures for funding agencies represent the total cost of medals as it is quite possible that national governing bodies and private sector sponsors may also contribute to the production process. Nonetheless, the examples illustrated in this section give an insight into how the analysis can be used once the data is sufficiently robust to enable like for like comparisons. In the same way that the measure of total medals won does not show the 'totality of achievement' (Section 4.4) so too Table 4.18 does not discriminate between the quality of medals won by sports. To overcome what we consider to be a methodological weakness, we have adapted Table 4.18 to illustrate the cost of medal points won by sport. Unfortunately, the UK national governing bodies of sport were not required to specify the hue of medals that they were targeting and thus it is not possible to compute the budgeted cost of points won.

Table 4.20: Cost of medal points won by UK Sport-funded sports (2004)

Sport Point	Funding € m	Gold (3)	Silver (2)	Bronze (1)	Total	Points	Cost per point € m
Swimming	9.49	-	-	2	2	2	4.75
Athletics	16.50	3	-	1	4	10	1.61
Rowing	15.48	1	2	1	4	8	1.90
Cycling	11.83	2	1	1	4	9	1.31
Modern Pentathlon	2.92	-	-	1	1	1	2.92
Canoeing	6.86	-	1	2	3	4	1.75
Sailing	10.51	2	1	2	5	10	1.02
Diving	2.04	-	1	-	1	2	1.02
Equestrian	4.67	1	1	1	3	6	0.73
Archery	0.44	-	-	1	1	1	0.44
Gymnastics	6.13	-	-	-	0	0	-
Judo	5.11	-	-	-	0	0	-
Triathlon	3.80	-	-	-	0	0	-
Shooting	2.19	-	-	-	0	0	-
Taekwondo	0.88	-	-	-	0	0	-
Weightlifting	0.15	-		-	0	0	-
Total	98.99	9	7	12	28	53	1.90

When adjusted for the quality of medals, the average actual cost of medal points won by Great Britain and Northern Ireland in Athens 2004 was € 1.9m across the portfolio of sports. Again there are considerable disparities by sport with swimming being the notable high outlier at € 4.75m per medal point. The bronze medal won in Modern Pentathlon although below average cost per medal in Table 4.18 (€ 2.92m) is shown to be an expensive medal to have won when standardised on a points basis, i.e. € 2.92m for one point compared with an average cost of € 1.90m per point. In the case of Flanders the average cost per point is € 6.64m because the two medals won were both bronze.

A further way in which we examine the National Audit Office data is on the priority status of various sports. For some time, UK Sport operated a classification system based on various factors such as success in the past, likelihood of winning medals in the future and public demand for success in that sport. When the expenditure and performance of the priority groups that applied at the time of the 2004 Olympics are aggregated, some interesting findings emerge as shown in Table 4.21.

Table 4.21: The efficiency investments in UK Sport-funded sports (2004)

Sport Priority	Sport	Investment (€ m)	Medals Targeted	Medals Won	Target Accuracy	Cost per Medal (€ m)
1	Athletics, Sailing, Rowing, Cycling	54.31	18	17	94%	3.194
2	Swimming, Canoeing, Judo, Equestrian, Pentathlon, Shooting	31.24	12	9	75%	3.471
3	Gymnastics, Triathlon, Diving	11.97	7	1	14%	11.970
4	Taekwondo, Archery, Weightlifting	1.31	6	1	17%	1.310
Totals		**98.99**	**43**	**28**	**65%**	**3.540**

Table 4.21 reveals that as a whole, Priority 1 sports have an average cost of €3.194m per medal which is below the portfolio average of €3.54m. Perhaps of greater note is that there is a near perfect match between medals targeted and medals won (94%). By contrast, priority 3 sports have a high average cost per medal €11.97m and a low success rate (14%) in winning the number of medals targeted. These findings would seem to endorse the importance of nations investing in 'focus' sports in which there is a track record of prior success and a reasonable probability of future success, rather than spreading resources thinly across all 28 Olympic sports.

Assuming that the process for allocating resources towards medal winning success is rational, Tables 4.18, 4.19, 4.20 and 4.21 enable informed decisions to be made as to the acceptability of the cost or value for money of investments.

Value for money assessments can be made in advance of events by linking the level of investment required to the targeted cost of medals. Thus although Table 4.21 reveals that the actual cost of medals in Priority 4 sports was € 1.310m, the budgeted cost was € 0.218m. Therefore, the single medal won in Priority 4 sports cost six times as much as the budgeted cost. This sort of analysis complements the portfolio of effectiveness measures reviewed earlier and confirms that medal-based measures are but limited measures of the rounded performance of an elite athlete production system.

An arguably more useful application of the analysis in Table 4.18 is transnational comparisons, that is, how much are other nations investing to achieve a given level of success? It follows that if certain nations are using essentially the same elite athlete production system, then in addition to looking at effectiveness of a system we also need to consider efficiency at the same time. Currently, although we have outlined a methodology which will enable such comparisons to be made, the data upon which such calculations depend are not sufficiently valid or reliable to enable more detailed analysis at this stage. Nonetheless, the crucial point remains that monitoring and evaluation are integral components of strategic planning processes. The financial efficiency measures outlined in this section are likely to play an increasingly important role in influencing elite athlete production systems and related decision making in the future.

4.10   Conclusions

In order to identify a link between performance and policy, the initial purpose of this chapter was to propose an objective performance ranking for the sample nations. This has proven to be an ambitious task because the sporting priorities of individual nations vary along a continuum of 'diversity' to 'priority'. It would be naive to suggest that there is a single performance measure or model that can be applied uniformly to all nations. Some nations invest in a broad portfolio of Olympic and non-Olympic sports (UK and the Netherlands); some might focus more narrowly on Olympic sports (Italy); others on summer Olympic sports and others again on winter Olympic sports (Canada and Norway). The purest form of comparison is on a sport by sport basis and this is identified as a priority for future research. We can conclude however that the ranking of nations in any sporting performance index will be a function of the portfolio of sports chosen and the priority of those sports to individual nations. It is not possible to rank the sporting performance of the six sample nations meaningfully without regard to these factors.

In addition to raising the issues linked to quantifying and ranking the performance of the sample nations, this chapter also highlights four issues that may have an impact on how policies towards elite sport development systems are monitored and evaluated in the future. These four key points are discussed in turn below.

First, if elite sport development systems are viewed as a strategic management process (Figure 4.1) then integral components of the process must be monitoring and control. The importance of monitoring and control can be appreciated by two key points. First, competition for success in elite sport is increasing. More nations are adopting strategic approaches towards the development of elite athletes and as a result an increasing number of nations have developed genuine medal winning capability. Second, the resource implication for elite sport is considerable. In the UK, even before the Government announced more money for elite sport on the back of London's successful bid for the 2012 Olympics, UK Sport was committed to a €143m investment in elite sport during the Beijing Olympiad, an increase of €20m on the sum invested in the Athens Olympiad. When such large sums of money are involved, there will be a natural desire – if not a requirement - to measure how actual performance compares with planned performance.

Second, traditional measures such as medal tables have a function in terms of being easily understood rankings of actual performance. However, as indicated in Tables 4.8 and 4.9 it is possible for medal based measures of performance to give conflicting results concerning a nation's performance. This type of ambiguity does not help Performance Directors whose future funding and jobs may well be dependent on delivering a specified level of success. To overcome this problem, market share is identified as being a standardised measure which enables meaningful time series analysis to be conducted. Furthermore, the factors by which market share can be altered are controllable by the management and quality of elite athlete production models. The issue of controllability contrasts favourably with measures such as medal table ranking where it is demonstrated that it is possible for a nation's ranking to improve whilst simultaneously experiencing a deterioration in medals won, points and market share.

Third, time is identified as an important ingredient in an elite sports development system. Those nations which have been investing in elite sport for the longest tend to be more successful than those nations whose engagement with the process is more recent. For this reason, and the reason that medals won cannot always serve as a measure of distance travelled, it is important that the elite sport programme of given sports is evaluated using more comprehensive measures of success. These might include measures ranging from the number of athletes qualifying to take part in an event through to the narrowing of the gap between national records and medal winning performance.

Fourth, as more nations adopt essentially the same methods of elite athlete development a further measure of performance is the efficiency of the production process. As has been shown in the case of Great Britain and Northern Ireland, and to a lesser extent Belgium, it is possible to attach costs to outputs so that calculations such as 'cost per medal' can be computed. Thus it is possible to assess not only the efficacy of investment decisions but also the financial efficiency. Whilst the use of economics and management accounting to evaluate performance in elite sport may be anathema to sports purists; the reality is that increasing competition for medals and increased investment requirements for elite sport programmes will lead to greater rather than less scrutiny in the future.

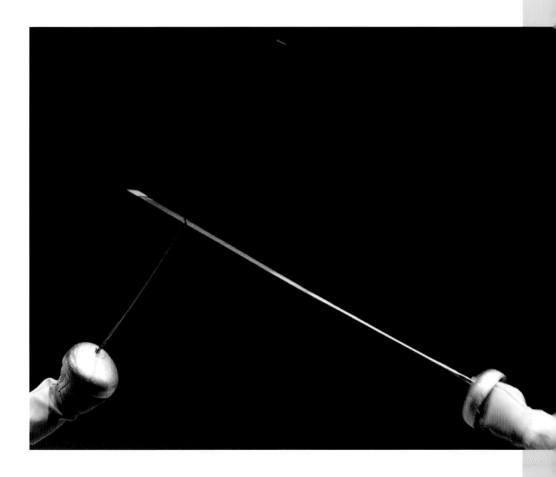

Chapter 5:

A comparative analysis of elite sports systems in the six sample nations

Introduction

This chapter is concerned with the evaluation of elite sports policies in the sample nations making use of two sources of information: the overall policy questionnaire and the elite sports climate survey filled in by athletes, coaches and Performance Directors. Both surveys try to measure inputs and throughputs. The basic framework of our analysis consists of nine sports policy factors, or "pillars", that are commonly considered to be important for international sporting success. The model is based on an extended literature review of success determinants in sport, different sources of elite sports systems, completed with an experimental test with Flemish athletes, coaches and Performance Directors as explained in Chapter 2. Given that some features of successful nations as defined by Oakley and Green (2001b) and Clumpner (1994) cannot easily be quantified, they can be subjectively assessed by their primary users, in this case the athletes and their coaches, which was the aim of the elite sports climate survey. As a consequence of underdeveloped sports policies in any of the nine pillars a gap may arise between the expected and delivered service. The consequence may be dissatisfaction, which in turn may negatively influence the performance of athletes. This theory is known as the 'gap' model in service quality literature by Parasuraman, Zeithalm & Berry (1985). The concept is also widely accepted in the "effectiveness" literature, where it is stated that the primary stakeholders should be involved (Chelladurai, 2001; Papadimitriou & Taylor, 2000). This research aims to evaluate both content of elite sports policies and perceived quality. However, with the latter we must bear in mind that such assessments are subjective and may be linked to the personal circumstances of the respondents.

The data gathered from the two types of survey allowed us to define measurable criteria for each pillar. We used a five-point scale to assess each nation's performance against each criterion and aggregated these scores in order to produce one overall rating for each pillar. A total percentage score was then calculated taking into account missing data as some nations were unable to provide all the requested information. When two thirds of the necessary data were unavailable, scores were not calculated. For each pillar, nations' ratings are presented in a colour-coded format as shown below. This colour coding scheme is discussed for each pillar.

Evaluation	
Policy area very well developed	
Good level of development	
Moderate level of development	
Limited development	
Little or no development	

Further details regarding the methodology of this scoring system, as part of a Ph.D. study, are provided in appendix two.

Overall, over 100 criteria were defined and measured. Taking into account all the limitations summed up in chapter 3 regarding different response groups, a prudent attempt has been made to develop a measurement system for evaluating elite sports systems in six nations (seven regions).

This research methodology is experimental. The results proposed here should be seen as a pilot study for further evaluation. It was the aim in this research to present a methodology and a list of criteria for each pillar that can be used for further research with more nations.

5.1 Pillar 1: Financial support

Comparative analysis

	CAN	FL	IT	NI	NOR	UK	WAL
Expenditure on sport at national level	◐	◐	○	○	◐	○	◐
Funding of National Governing Bodies	◐	●	○	○	●	◐	●

key	
◐	high level of investment
○	fairly high level of investment
○	moderate level of investment
◐	fairly low level of investment
●	low level of investment

Selected and available criteria

National expenditure on sport
- Total national expenditure on sport (cash terms)
- Total national expenditure on sport (per head of population)
- Total Government expenditure on sport (as a proportion of total Government expenditure)
- Increase / decrease in total national expenditure on sport 1999-2003
- National expenditure on elite sport (cash terms)
- National expenditure on elite sport (per head of population)
- National expenditure on elite sport (as a proportion of total national expenditure on sport
- Increase / decrease in national expenditure on elite sport since 1999-2003

Financial support for national governing bodies
- Total financial support for NGBs (cash terms)
- Total financial support for NGBs (per head of population)
- Total financial support for NGBs (average funding per governing body)
- Financial support for NGBs: elite sport (cash terms)
- Financial support for NGBs: elite sport (as a proportion of total financial support for governing bodies)
- Financial support for NGBs: elite sport (average funding per governing body)

5.1.1 Concept and definition

Making cross-national comparisons of expenditure on sport is a notoriously difficult exercise. To keep our analysis as simple and consistent as possible, we have chosen to look just at public expenditure on sport at national level – that is, expenditure derived from central government and/or national lotteries. We have, as far as possible, also sought to ensure consistency in terms of what the participating nations include within their definition of public expenditure. While we acknowledge that in most nations expenditure by local government and/or the private sector is greater than that provided by national government, we found that data in this respect was either not available or not sufficiently comparable. It should also be pointed out that the ratings we have worked out in this area are entirely an indication of the relative investment made (in 2003) by each nation in our sample. So, whereas here the UK scores highly in terms of financial support provided to national governing bodies, there may well be other nations not included in our sample which invest considerably more in this regard.

Total sport and elite sport expenditure in each participating nation as at 2003 is set out in appendices four & five. As might reasonably be expected, in absolute cash terms total national expenditure on sport is greatest in the United Kingdom (€610m p.a.) and Italy (€273m p.a.) i.e. the two nations with the largest populations. In Italy it should be noted that the budget includes funding for sport facilities and nine military sports clubs. When we compare spending in relation to population size, however, a different picture emerges: Norway comes out highest with total sports spending of €28.6 per head of the population, followed by Flanders with €14.3 and Wallonia with €9.3. Canada (at €2.1 per head) and Italy (€4.7 per head) are at the bottom end of the range. However, it should be noted that the Provinces in Canada are very autonomous in sport and most of the expenditure is probably made at regional level. Precise figures are not known as there is no national co-ordination of expenditure by province. Government expenditure on sport expressed as a proportion of all government expenditure is also highest in Norway and Flanders – i.e. 0.32% and 0.17% respectively.

When we compare expenditure levels in 2003 with those in 1999, we find that spending increased in most nations, ranging from 30% in Norway to 90% in the Netherlands. Wallonia showed a status quo (€40.8 million) for this period but an increase of 25% is noticed afterwards (in 2006). In Italy, however, it appears that total sports spending fell in cash terms over this period, primarily the result of a decline in revenues from sport-related gambling. This is also the reason why, over the last four years, the Italian government has provided an additional financial contribution (c. €60 to €125 million per year) when state intervention prior to this was minimal. Only in 2005 has the state for the first time agreed to support the NOC with a fixed amount (approximately €450 million per year), regardless of the financial support it receives from the lotteries.

Four of the participating nations (the United Kingdom, Flanders, the Netherlands and Norway) also increased their investment in elite sport between 1999 and 2003, with budgets more than doubling in the UK, Wallonia and Flanders. Figures for 1999 were not available for Canada or Italy. In terms of absolute expenditure on elite sport, Italy (€125m per annum (estimated)) and the UK (€90m p.a.) again appear to be the biggest spenders, with the Netherlands in third place – albeit, at €41.6m p.a., some distance behind.

Differences in the funding of National Governing Bodies (NGBs) generally correspond with differences in other areas of sports expenditure. Italy (€140m p.a.) heads the UK (€95m p.a.) in terms of its overall funding of NGBs, with the Netherlands (at €66m p.a.) again in third place. Italy also has the highest level of funding per NGB. However, our figures indicate that the UK (€50m p.a.) invests nearly twice as much as Italy in support of NGBs' elite sport activities. The UK also provides the highest average level of support for each NGB that is funded at the elite level (on average € 1.25m per NGB). Flanders and Norway provide the lowest levels of elite sport funding per NGB. A detailed table of financial support for NGBs is provided in appendix 5.

5.1.2 Key findings

One clear point emerging from the European nations in the sample is the homogeneity of the funding model for sport. It would appear that accepted practice is for sport to be funded via a combination of Exchequer (or Treasury) and lottery funding. As far as central governments are concerned, the use of lottery funds to support sport is classed as being 'off balance sheet' funding. This means that financial support for sport is not entirely derived from direct and indirect taxation. The only difference in the application of the sport funding model in each nation is the proportion of funds derived from Exchequer and lottery funding. In Italy, until 2003, state funding of sport was relatively low (46%) and lottery funding was high (54%), whereas in smaller nations such as the Netherlands and Flanders state funding of sport is considerably higher (65%+) and lotteries are relied on less (<35%). In Norway, the profit from lotteries is regarded as public money because the shareholding company "Norsk Tipping" (lotteries) is state-owned.

Looked at in the round, our analysis of public expenditure on sport shows that, among the participating nations, three – Italy, the UK and the Netherlands – stand out as the most serious investors in elite sport. Flanders and Norway both appear to give sport generally a certain degree of priority as an area of public policy and spend the highest per capita sums on sport of all nations: however, these attributes do not extend into the field of elite sport, where their spending accounts for less than 12% of total sports expenditure. While Flanders and Wallonia have the highest increase in elite sport expenditures (+115% and 182% respectively) since 1999, this is still relatively low, both in absolute and relative terms, compared to the other nations. The Flemish government has committed to an increased budget for elite sport of €15m p.a. by 2009, which will be 17% of the overall government funding on sport.

While Canada is the nation within our sample which appears to spend the greatest proportion of its national sports budget (55%) on elite sport, an annual allocation of €38m p.a. leaves it still someway behind the top three nations in terms of cash spending. It is likely that Canada is the nation that suffers most in our analysis from the omission of sub-national expenditure data (it appears that a considerable investment is made in sport generally, and in elite sport specifically, at provincial level in Canada). However, following the federal budget announcement in February 2005, in which the Canadian Government provided a funding base of €100 million for sport (an increase of €31m, compared with 2003), it also seems likely that national investment in Canadian high performance sport is set to rise. Indeed, with the 2010 Winter Olympic and Paralympic Games being hosted in Vancouver, we are aware that there is considerable interest in Canada in seeing its athletes do well, while at the same time developing a stronger system that will improve and sustain results over time.

Italy, the UK and the Netherlands are the three nations which we have identified as the best performing nations in international competition in summer sports. Moreover, they are three nations whom we have identified as having taken, over different time periods, a clear strategic approach to the development of elite sport. In Italy, this dated back to 1942 when the Italian National Olympic Committee (CONI) was given the rights to sports-related gambling profits. These monies have been used to support state, regional and local level networks of elite athlete development. The Netherlands has invested heavily in elite sport following the merger of the National Olympic Committee and National Sports Federation in 1993 to create NOC*NSF. Since 1997, the UK developed and invested in its World Class Performance Programmes and associated athlete support services with the express intention of addressing the poor performance of Team GB in the 1996 Atlanta Olympics.

When output is measured in winter Olympic sports we find that the balance of power shifts in favour of Norway and Canada, which are two nations that invest relatively modest amounts of money in elite sport in absolute terms. The specific competency of Norway and Canada in winter sports may in part be explained by two factors. First, performance in the winter Olympic Games is more dependent on nations' natural environments (that is, mountains and snow). Second, winter sports generally are often more 'market oriented' and therefore less dependent on public expenditures on sport. However, neither of these two explanatory variables can be influenced significantly by policy.

For all nations reliant on lottery receipts for the funding of sport, fluctuating levels of public support for lotteries can cause unpredictable income levels and thereby introduce uncertainty in the planning for elite sport. If NGBs are not insulated from such fluctuations, as they have been in Italy, the end result is shorter planning horizons and the adoption of short term behaviour rather than planning for the longer term. In addition to the 'cushioning' provided by the Italian government to compensate for falling gambling receipts, lessons can also be learnt from other nations in the sample where NGBs are given four year planning cycles i.e. from one Olympiad to the next.

5.2 Pillar 2:
Integrated approach to policy development

Comparative analysis

	CAN	FL	IT	NL	NOR	UK	WAL
Evaluation	NA	○	◉	○	○	○	○
Assessment by athletes and coaches			no assessment on this pillar				

key ○ policy area very well developed
○ good level of development
○ moderate level of development
◐ fairly low level of development
● low level of development
NA data not available

Selected and available criteria

Policies at national level
- Organisation of sports and policies
    - Public sector efficiency (source: European Central Bank, 2003)
    - Specific Ministry of Sport
    - An organisation at national level with specific responsibilities for elite sport as a core task
    - Coordination of expenditures at national level (horizontal)
    - Coordination of expenditures at regional level (vertical)
- Provision of services to NGBs
        to develop their management capability
- Number of recognised and funded NGBs
- Number of NGBs funded for elite sport purposes
- Information received from NGBs by athletes and coaches
- Athlete representation within NGBs

Assessment by athletes and coaches
Satisfaction of athletes and coaches with regards to:
- Athletes' and coaches' satisfaction levels on the supply of information from NGBs
- involvement in the policy-making process of NGBs

5.2.1 Concept and definition

The second pillar concerns the organisation and structure of sport in the sample nations. At a strategic level it is our view that for nations to have a realistic chance of elite sporting success, an appropriate lead needs to be given by governments. Operationally, we believe that a coherent structure is a prerequisite for the efficient use of resources. According to Oakley and Green (2001b) and Clumpner (1994), it is especially important to delineate clearly the responsibilities of different agencies; to ensure there is effective communication between them; and to simplify administration.

It is difficult to 'measure' these determinants other than via a fairly broad brush approach. Based on a limited number of criteria in this respect (we are, after all, more interested in the underlying policy process than structures themselves), our general view is that the basic structures of elite sport at national and regional levels are reasonably similar in all of the participating nations. Background information on the sport policy structures and policies in the sample nations is provided in appendix three.

We took as a starting point for our analysis, a broad assessment of public sector efficiency undertaken by the European Central Bank in 23 industrialised nations (Afonso, Schuknecht, & Tanzi V., 2003). Efficiency indicators were developed in administration, education, health, infrastructure, distribution, stability and the economy. In this research, Japan, Switzerland, Australia and the United States emerged as the most efficient nations. The ranking for the participating nations in this survey was as follows: Norway (6th), United Kingdom (9th), Canada (11th), the Netherlands, (16th), Belgium (20th) and Italy (23rd). The research indicated that smaller nations in terms of population in general scored higher. Belgium is the exception here, with a relatively poor efficiency score.

The greatest emphasis in this pillar was put on the coordination of elite sports policies and expenditures. UK Sport and Olympiatoppen in Norway are responsible only for elite sport at national level, whereas NOC*NSF (the Netherlands), Bloso (Flanders), Adeps (Wallonia), CONI (Italy) and Sport Canada also have responsibilities for general sport development. This may lead to tension between the development of sport for all and elite sport. Furthermore, we looked at how elite sport expenditure and policies are centrally coordinated at a national level, horizontally (between different national agencies) and vertically (national versus regional). As Clumpner (1994) states, "there must be an unbroken line of communication up through all levels of the system and a communication network that supports the system. Such a system would allow the athlete to continue in a straight line up through the system rather than force the athlete to switch back and forth between various sporting bodies" (1994, p 358).

The United Kingdom and Belgium have particularly complex political structures that can create difficulties in coordinating policy and allocating resources across their constituent nations or communities. In the United Kingdom, some sports are supported at a UK-level, others on a home nation basis (England, Scotland, Wales and Northern Ireland). Nevertheless, responsibilities are delineated transparently to ensure clarity of purpose and to avoid duplication. In Belgium (Flanders and Wallonia) there is a similarly complex structure whereby sport is predominantly a regional affair with no national policy other than from BOIC. Sport in Flanders and Wallonia is coordinated entirely independently which has led to a fragmentation

CHAPTER 5

of resources and responsibilities. Furthermore, even within Flanders or Wallonia, several organisations have responsibilities in elite sport. The establishment of a steering group in Flanders (in 2003) to coordinate elite sport expenditures and activities has been one of the most important policy improvements during the last decade. However, regardless of this complex state structure the 'policy area well developed' score for the UK indicates that at meso level it is possible for a field such as sport to score well on pillar 2.

In Canada sports policies and partly elite sports policies is to a large extent decentralised at the provincial / territory level. Green and Houlihan (2005) noted the problem in Canada of pressure to centralise on the one hand and resistance from peripheral regions, states, territories and provinces on the other hand. Centralisation does not necessarily mean that all actions take place at a national level, but in elite sport policies particularly, there is a need for national coordination and an inventory of regional provision in order to maximise the services delivered to athletes, coaches and National Governing Bodies.

In specifically sporting terms, we focused our attention on the support that is given to national governing bodies of sport ("federations"). In most nations, it is, after all, the federations that are responsible for running and developing individual sports. Unsurprisingly, we found that, in all participating nations, federations receive some level of financial support from the government or national, non-governmental sports organisations. Some nations, such as the Netherlands, support a broad spectrum of sports for elite performances, 63 in total, including non-Olympic sports such as billiards, bridge, and chess. As was pointed out by several authors it may be more efficient in elite sport to target the resources on a relatively small number of sports through identifying those that have a real chance of success at world level (Wells, 1991; Oakley and Green, 2001; Clumpner, 1996). This strategy was followed by the former communist nations and in Australia. In Flanders 26 NGBs receive funds for elite sport, in Norway 30, in Wallonia 36 and in the UK 40 (see appendix 6).

We have also examined the services provided to federations in order to support their talent development programmes and to ensure they are managed on a professional basis. The Dutch and UK systems are perhaps the most striking. NOC*NSF, the Netherlands national Olympic Committee and national sports federation, has appointed seven elite sport account managers who are responsible for the provision of information and advice to federations on elite sport policies, long term planning and funding applications. Federations can also obtain advice from four technical advisers and one technical adviser on talent development, to develop "World Class Performance Programmes". In the United Kingdom, UK Sport offers a similar range of expert support and, in 2001, set up a Modernisation Programme to help national governing bodies of sport become more efficient and effective in all aspects of their work. Although at the time of writing (2006) the Programme no longer exists as a separate funding stream, the money remains available to support governing bodies in the delivery of their "world class" programmes.

In Norway, Olympiatoppen has a pool of coaches, medical staff and consultants to provide advice on organisational aspects of National Governing Bodies. There are similar initiatives in Canada, with 125 staff and several consultants working in Sport Canada, to provide guidance to NSOs. It appears that federation services amongst our participating nations are least well developed in Italy, Wallonia and Flanders. However, there is some evidence that this situation is now changing in Flanders, which explains its higher score on this criterion.

The management capabilities of governing bodies were partly evaluated by the athletes and coaches in the elite sports climate survey. Although only coaches responded to questionnaires in Italy and only athletes in Norway and Canada, the findings were generally consistent with the previous results. Athletes and coaches in the Netherlands, UK, Norway and Canada pointed out that they received information from governing bodies on subjects like nutrition, selection criteria, doping, training and competition plans, travel plans, scientific research and in most cases they were satisfied with this information. Flanders again remains below the international average. Although more than two thirds of the Dutch and British coaches felt they had sufficient involvement in policy matters, athletes were less satisfied in this respect. In Canada, one of the key changes undertaken recently was a minimum athlete representation on decision-making committees of national sport federations, known as the 20% solution (Thibault & Babiak, 2005). Although this criterion was not evaluated by Canadian athletes, it appears in the elite sports climate survey, that 10 out of 11 sports federations in Canada have an athletes' commission, and 76% of the athletes are members. This was only 10% in Flanders, 21% in Norway and 35% in the Netherlands. These figures are consistent with athletes' satisfaction concerning their involvement in National Governing Body policy.

5.2.2 Key findings

The major point of note is that there is little variation in the scores achieved by the sample nations against Pillar 2, thus, in this respect, endorsing the point made by Oakley and Green (2001b) about the increasing homogeneity of nations' elite sport development systems. The positive scores achieved by Norway, the Netherlands and the United Kingdom can in part be explained by the finding that, in each of these nations, both the government and the national sports organisation appear to be fully committed to the support and development of sport at elite level and there is a high degree of coordination of expenditures and activities. In the UK, there is a highly-developed support system for National Governing Bodies, which helps to explain the high score.

Another key factor in the UK, Norway and to a lesser extent the Netherlands has been the occurrence of a "focussing event" which has acted as a catalyst for significant and sustained investment in elite sport. For the UK, this was the poor British performance in the 1996 Atlanta Olympics, when it won just one gold medal. Since 1997 there has been considerable government commitment to put in place world class systems for elite sport development, which have been backed with the requisite resources to lift the UK from 36th place in the Atlanta medal table to 10th place in both Sydney and Athens. This UK investment in elite sport was also positively endorsed by athletes and a small sample of coaches. In the Netherlands NOC*NSF merged in 1993 and invested heavily in elite sport after the relative failures in Albertville (1992) and Lillehammer (1994) compared with Calgary 1998. In the run up to Sydney 2000, the Netherlands aimed to become one of the top 10 performing nations in the world. In Norway Olympiatoppen was found after poor results during the Winter Olympics in 1984. While Norway won no gold medals in 1988, by the Albertville Games of 1992, it improved to win nine gold medals, six silver and five bronze and received additional funding in preparation for hosting the Lillehammer Games in 1994. Since the Sydney Olympics in 2000, Olympiatoppen has developed a range of sports science and medicine support services.

The same theory may also be applied to Canada. With the 2010 Winter Olympic and Paralympic Games being hosted in Vancouver, the sporting community has called for a longer-term strategy that focuses on ensuring continued improvements in Canada's international results in 2010 and beyond. Funding will facilitate the creation of a generic national Long Term Athlete Development (LTAD) model, as is already present in some sports in the UK. Furthermore with the elections at the beginning of 2006, for the first time sport has become the responsibility of a Cabinet Minister.

5.3   Pillar 3: Participation in sport (organised and unorganised)

Comparative analysis

	CAN	FL	IT	NI	NOR	UK	WALL
Evaluation	○	○	○	○	◉	○	○
Assessment by athletes and coaches	NA	◐	◐	○	○	NA	NA

key		
	○	policy area very well developed
	○	good level of development
	○	moderate level of development
	◐	fairly low level of development
	●	low level of development
	NA	data not available

Selected and available criteria

1. Physical Education

Nursery
- National statutory amount of minimum time for PE
- Average amount of time actually allocated to PE (in minutes per week)

Primary education and secondary education
- National statutory amount of minimum time for PE
- Average amount of time actually allocated to PE (in minutes per week)
- Existence / regularity of extra curricular competitions

2. Sport participation

- Participation in sport at least once a week
- Total number of sport club members
- Sport club members per head of population
- Percentage of population participating in a sports or outdoor club
- Total number of registered sport clubs
- Existence of quality stimulation projects in sport clubs

5.3.1 Concept and definition

Although there is much information on the amount of physical education (PE) and the levels of sport participation in the various nations involved in this study, international comparisons are hard to make. The difficulty with respect to PE is that its organisation varies not only between but also within each nation, often from school to school, which makes it hard to determine and compare the amount of time devoted to PE in each nation. We therefore confined ourselves in this study to the statutory minimum amount of time for PE in nursery, primary and secondary education in each nation, and the weekly average amount of time as reported by our researchers in the overall questionnaire on the basis of various nation-specific sources. Extra curricular competitions are another criterion. However limited data were available from the sample nations on the number of pupils and schools that participate regularly in such competitions.

It is also widely recognised in sports research that the comparability of sport participation surveys is problematic if the methodology and questionnaires have not been harmonised. For the purpose of this international-comparative study, we therefore did not make use of individual surveys on sports participation carried out separately in the various nations. Instead, we looked for an international standardised survey, held in or around 2003 in as many as possible of the nations participating in our study. This turned out to be the Eurobarometer of 2003 and the European Social Survey of 2002 with questions on sport participation and club membership respectively. For other information – i.e. the total number of sport club members, the total number of registered sport clubs and the extent to which quality management in sport clubs has been introduced – we relied on the overall sports policy questionnaire.

5.3.2 Key findings

The most solid foundation for PE can be found in Flanders and Norway. Only in these nations, is there a statutory minimum time for PE in nursery, primary and secondary education. However, the average amount of time actually allocated to PE in these nations seems to be quite similar to that in most other nations, namely between one and two hours a week. In nursery school PE is part of the curriculum only in Flanders, Norway and the Netherlands. Overall we conclude that, although the school and PE systems vary from nation to nation, the position of PE does not differ substantially between the nations considered in this study. Italy is the exception to this rule as the amount of attention given to PE within both nursery and primary education is determined by the head teacher.

Similar results to Italy can be found in Canada, where a national statutory amount of PE is lacking because of the autonomy of Provinces in education. Some Provinces have a minimum time for PE, others do not. Even within a given Province there are many Boards of Education that operate relatively independently. Although a decentralised policy may be a solution for large nations such as Canada, it is our view that even in a decentralised policy, there should be a degree of coherence nationally. Consequently it should also be noted that Canada has a lot of 'non available' answers in this pillar.

Only in Flanders and Wallonia are there regular extra-school competitions organised centrally by SVS (the foundation for Flemish school sports) and A.F.F.S.S. (the Association Francophone des Fédérations Sportives Scolaires) who are both funded by Bloso and Adeps. In Canada and the UK school sport varies by school and region. However, since the year 2000, a government initiative in the UK has seen the appointment of 600 School Sports Coordinators to help provide an extended range of opportunities for intra and extra mural sport in state schools.

In addition, a planned cohort of up to 400 specialist sports colleges (there were 283 in operation as at September 2004) will form an important part of a planned, coordinated and integrated model of elite sport development in the UK (Green & Houlihan, 2005). In Canada the university sector plays a particularly significant role in the talent development process. Canadian Interuniversity Services (CIS) represents over 12,000 athletes and 550 full and part-time coaches who are training and working in Canadian universities. Furthermore the Canadian Colleges Athletic Association (CCAA) is the sole coordinating body for college sport comprising 9,000 in-tercollegiate athletes, 700 coaches and 150 sport administrators in total (Sport Canada, 2006).

With respect to sports participation, Italy lags behind the other nations on several criteria. This finding is consistent with international comparative studies on sport participation in Europe, which lead to the conclusion that people from northern Europe participate more often in sport and with greater intensity than people from southern Europe (see the results of the COMPASS-project [http://w3.uniroma1.it/compass] and Van Bottenburg, Rijnen & Van Sterkenburg, 2005). The latter study also concludes that sport in the context of sports clubs is particularly prevalent in the north-western part of Europe.

On the basis of our literature review, we stated in chapter two of this report that a broad base of sport participation is not always an essential condition for elite sports success, but may influence success to a large extent because of the continuous supply of young talent. It was shown by Van Bottenburg (2003) that elite sporting success is only significantly correlated with sport participation when sport is 'intensive and competitive'. From this perspective, we can conclude that most sample nations have the same potential in relative terms (percentage of sport participants). However in absolute terms, Canada, Italy, and the United Kingdom have a comparative advantage, as they have a greater number of sports participants and registered sports club members than the other sample nations. These nations can fish for talent in a larger pool of sports participants and sport clubs than Flanders, the Netherlands, Norway, and Wallonia.

As most athletes find their roots in sports clubs, this pillar refers not only to the number of sport participants but also to the quality delivered at club level. Green and Houlihan (2005) refer to Tihanyi that "it is much too late to develop Olympians at the level of the training centres. This process must be incubated, nurtured and brought to fruition at the club level" (2001, p29). Although quality in sport clubs is definitely a criterion that needs to be explored more in depth on a sport by sport basis, some nations have set up national projects to stimulate quality management in sports clubs. An example of this can be found in Flanders, where subsidy criteria for National Governing Bodies are partly based on initiatives for increasing quality in sports clubs. Some sports, such as gymnastics, korfball, football and hockey have developed a specific total quality measurement system with the aim of delivering quality labels for their clubs and accompanied with necessary consultancy. Another example is IKSport (Integral Quality in Sports clubs), which was designed to introduce "Total Quality Management" in sports clubs in Flanders and the Netherlands.

In conclusion the key finding of this section is that Italy scores less than the other nations because of its lack of coordination in PE and fewer sport club members. This latter item may be seen as the most important in relation to elite sporting success because in most nations talented athletes are mainly selected from an organised and competitive sporting environment.

5.4   Pillar 4:
Talent identification and development system

Comparative analysis

	CAN	FL	IT	NI	NOR	UK	WAL
Evaluation	◑	○	●	○	○	◑	◑
Assessment by athletes & coaches	NA	◑	○	○	○	NA	●

key	
◌	policy area very well developed
○	good level of development
○	moderate level of development
◑	fairly low level of development
●	low level of development
NA	data not available

Selected and available criteria

Talent Identification & Development

Stage 1: Talent identification
• A system-related talent selection process (non sport specific) is available
Stage 2: Talent development
• National coordinated system and financial support for the combination of elite sports and studies: secondary education level
• National coordinated system and financial support for the combination of elite sports and studies: higher education level
• Provision of information and support services to national sport federations to develop talent programmes
• Nature of extra attention young athletes received from NGB (according to athletes)
• Nature of extra attention young athletes received from club (according to athletes)

Assessment by athletes and coaches
• Sufficient amount of extra attention provided during talent development (according to athletes & coaches)
• Satisfaction of athletes with extra attention received from club
• Satisfaction of athletes with extra attention received from NGB
• Age at which extra attention was received is considered appropriate (according to coaches)

5.4.1 Concept and definition

Bloom (1985) identified three phases in the development of young talent in sports (and arts and science):
(a) the initiation phase, in which young athletes get to know their sport and are identified as being talented;
(b) the development phase in which athletes become more dedicated to their sport, train more, and become more specialised, and
(c) the perfection phase, in which athletes reach their highest level of performance.

Wylleman, De Knop & Sillen (1998) add a fourth phase to the three points above, namely the discontinuation phase when an athlete's competitive career has ended. Our discussion of Pillar 4 will be divided into two sections looking separately at talent identification and development. The area of athletic and post career support will be covered in Pillar 5. Each development domain has a number of transitions: at the academic and vocational level, the athletic level, the psychosocial and psychological level. Each transition requires 'special attention' during an athlete's elite sports career in order for their full potential to be realised (Wylleman & Lavallee, 2003).

5.4.2 Key findings
Stage 1: Talent identification

The majority of talent identification issues need to be analysed on a sport specific basis, as in most nations talented athletes are recruited from the existing participation base of a sport. A system-related scientific selection process, which aims to identify potential elite athletes from outside a sport's participant base, as was typical in the former communist nations (Riordan, 1991 & 1994; Fisher & Borms, 1990), is not used in any of the sample nations. Consequently there are almost no ratings for the sample nations against the talent identification phase. In two nations (Flanders & the Netherlands) the research was expanded by asking federations about their system of talent discovery in greater detail than on the policy questionnaire. This process revealed some additional and interesting findings. The Dutch federations were found to use more structured methods to recognise young talents than their Flemish counterparts. Furthermore the Flemish study also concluded that half of the federations believe that they begin their talent identification procedures too late and 10 federations (out of 26) estimated that they miss more than 25% of the young athletes who would be eligible for talent development initiatives. In smaller nations it is important to plan for talent identification in order to provide the system with as much raw material as possible (Rowe, 1994).

The Australian national Talent Search Program has hitherto been regard as the most developed system-related talent selection process (non sport specific) in use in the Western world. Each year approximately 10,000 young people (from 800 schools) around the age of 14 are introduced to the most physiologically appropriate sport of their choice. The more talented children are offered up to two years' intensive training, under professional guidance (Oakley and Green, 2001b). Thus far the system has been particularly successful in discovering international talent in athletics, cycling, weightlifting and women's rowing (Robinson, 1997).

In practice the combined scores for talent identification and *development* in this report are composed almost entirely of talent development ratings owing to the near absence of talent *identification* systems in the sample nations.

Stage 2: Talent development

Research has shown that, as a rule of thumb, roughly 8 to 10 years and 10,000 training hours are needed to become an expert in music or sport (Bloom, 1985; Grimbel, 1976; Starkes, 2000). Much of this investment of time and effort coincides with a talented person's secondary and tertiary education phases. In the talent development phase no nation is rated as having a 'good level of development' and Norway, the Netherlands and Flanders score relatively highly compared with the rest of the sample. The latter is largely because of the way in which all three nations provide nationally co-ordinated systems and financial support for talented athletes during the secondary phase of their education. They all share the important feature that the Ministry of Education has a legal framework by which to enable this combination of elite sport training and formal education. To a lesser extent Wallonia also has coordinated programmes but these are decentralised. In Canada a few initiatives are implemented at provincial level. It is estimated that six (out of ten) provinces make some arrangements for athletes involved in elite sport and academic study. Some advantages and disadvantages of the systems in secondary education in different nations are summed up below.

Table 5.1: Characteristics of elite sport and study systems in secondary education in the sample nations

	Strengths	Weaknesses
FL	"Elite sport schools" - centralised: the best athletes train together - finance through sports sector as well as educational sector - sportspecific coaching through federation, educational guidance through school - all ages (12-18 years old), depending on requirements of sport	- boarding school system - children away from home - recent initiative (1998)
NL	"LOOT-schools" - regional: close to home avoids home sickness - decentralised: many students/athletes - all ages	- best athletes do not train together in one centre - sport-specific coaching through sports clubs - sufficient expertise?
NOR	2 systems: centralised (15 Topp-Iddrettsgymnas) and decentralised - financed by Ministry of Education and Research & athletes recruited by federation - study results as a condition for the elite sports gymnasia - long tradition: since 1968	- Topp-Iddrettsgymnas are financed by athlete and are expensive - starts relatively late (15 years)
WAL	- decentralise: adaptation to athletes' individual needs - system totally coordinated by federation	- lack of logistic support to federations; have to arrange everything - themselves; lack of coordination; system limited to recognition by - ministry and some financial support; no study support

Flanders is the only nation with a central co-ordinated support system for athletes aged 18 and above (Tertiary education phase). Since 2003, student-athletes (young athletes who are not yet performing at elite level), have received a contract for a 'replacement salary' through Bloso (70% of the average salary levels for people who have the same qualifications) to allow for their increased cost of studying and training plus the delay they encounter in completing their studies. For high performance athletes a full salary (100%) salary is provided. The co-ordinator within the university receives € 3,000 per athlete in exchange for study support and the relevant NGB receives the sum of € 20,000 per student per academic year, for which NGBs are required to organize a comprehensive sport-specific curriculum. However, these elite sport and study systems have only been implemented recently, which explains the low rating given to talent development given by the Flemish athletes, as only 16 of 140 respondents had actually benefited from the secondary level system which was introduced in 1998.

The UK and Italy score relatively poorly on talent development primarily because of the lack of support for talented athletes at secondary school level. What this finding may be showing is that nations with larger populations and / or a good track record of success have, historically, taken a relatively relaxed approach to talent development, believing that talent will emerge naturally. In an increasingly competitive environment, the likelihood is that an approach of this type will no longer be sustainable and that more attention will need to be paid to this important phase of the athlete development process. In the case of the UK there have been significant recent changes in the approach to talent development techniques that athletes in the sample would not have experienced. Also, it appears that the NGBs in the UK generally receive a higher level of support and assistance for talent development activities from the national agencies than their Italian equivalents, which decide autonomously whether and how they spend their resources on talent identification and development. Although the Italian contributor points out that Italian NGB spending on talent-related work is generally quite high, it is for this reason that the UK rating is slightly higher than the Italian rating on this pillar. An efficiency analysis for the cost of medals by sport such as in the UK or in Flanders (see chapter 4) would allow more like for like comparisons.

In the Netherlands, two private initiatives have been launched at higher education level; namely, the Johan Cruyff College and University, and Randstad Topsport Academy. In Canada, Norway, the UK and Flanders athletes can obtain funding to assist with the cost of higher education. In Canada studies can be funded through the Athlete Assistance Programme (AAP) and in Norway free education can be offered via State intervention. In the United Kingdom, the government launched the Talented Athlete Scholarship Scheme (TASS) in 2004. This system is only operational in England and starts at the age of 16.

With the exception of Wallonia, all nations provided details relating to the extra support that young talented athletes received as they developed, from sources such as their clubs, national governing body or other sources. 'More intensive training' and 'clothes and equipment' were the most frequently cited extra provisions offered across all nations. Most of the extra provision was from clubs with further contributions coming from NGBs. Over 40% of athletes from Canada and the Netherlands reported receiving more intensive training from NGBs. Interestingly, 41% of the UK athletes had received mental coaching as a young talent, which differed significantly from the other nations. For the remaining nations this figure varied from 8% in Flanders, 12% in Norway to 17% in the Netherlands and Canada.

CHAPTER 5

Athletes were asked whether or not the support that they had received as young athletes was sufficient. The Norwegian athletes were the most satisfied (62%), followed by the Netherlands (55%), Canada (42%) and the United Kingdom (41%). The Wallonia score is noteworthy because 82% of the athletes felt that they received insufficient support. As in Flanders, student-athlete support systems have only recently been developed and only a few of the surveyed athletes have been able to make use of it. Coaches and Performance Directors were also asked to give their views on the current talent development provisions within their sport. Figure 5.1 summarises the satisfaction levels expressed by each nation. This differs to the athletes' survey where respondents were asked to reflect back on their experience as emerging talents - in many cases as long as ten years ago.

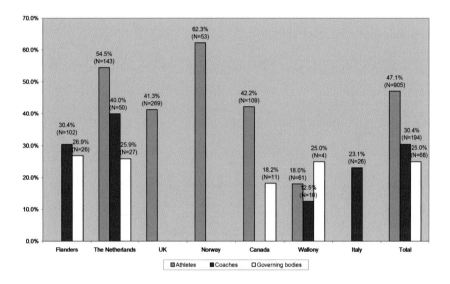

Figure 5.1: Percentage of athletes, national governing bodies and coaches indicating that sufficient support is offered to talented young athletes

Elite athletes were generally more satisfied than the coaches and the NGBs with the support provided to emerging talents. In the coaches' sample, Wallonia scores the lowest rating with 88% of respondents stating that insufficient support is offered to emerging talented athletes. In addition to the provision of information on what services were provided and at what age, athletes were asked to rate both club and NGB provision. These separate (club and NGB) satisfaction ratings were provided only by athletes from Flanders, Norway and the Netherlands. Norwegian athletes expressed greater levels of satisfaction with regard to club provision (68% described the provision as either good or sufficient) than NGB provision (33% good/reasonable). Athletes from Flanders also favoured club provision with 62% of athletes rating club provision as good/sufficient compared with 40% for NGB provision. Over half of the Dutch athletes expressed satisfaction with club provision (58%) and NGB provision (52%). The highest level of dissatisfaction was expressed by athletes from Flanders in relation to extra provision from NGBs (21% rated the provision as insufficient and 10% as poor).

In terms of the extent to which NGBs can receive non-financial support for talent development, there is guidance given to the NGBs in the Netherlands via the NOC*NSF and in Norway via the NOC/Olympiatoppen. It appears that in Italy, the United Kingdom and Canada support for talent development is mainly confined to financial support. However, the UK and Canada have both developed a Long Term Athlete Development programme which is specific to given sports. The seven-stage Canadian model for Long-Term Athlete Development (LTAD) is an overview of a training, competition, and recovery programmes based on developmental age rather than chronological age. It is athlete centred, coach driven and supported with administration, sport science and sponsor back-up. Athletes who progress through LTAD experience training and competition programmes that consider their biological age and training ages in creating periodised plans specific to their development needs. In Flanders non-financial support for talent development was considered a weakness but has recently been made a priority in the elite sport action plan for 2004-2009. In Canada, while grass roots development is the specific responsibility of the provincial federations, as each of the 10-12 independent bodies is asked to work co-operatively with the national body.

5.5 Pillar 5:
Athletic and post career support

Comparative analysis

	CAN	FL	IT	NI	NOR	UK	WAL
Evaluation	○	◉	○	◉	○	◉	◉
Assessment by athletes	○	○	NA	◉	○	NA	NA

key
- policy area very well developed
- good level of development
- moderate level of development
- fairly low level of development
- low level of development

NA   data not available

NB: Italy and Wallonia supplied data on relatively few criteria

Selected and available criteria
Stage 1: athletic career
• The number of athletes in the top 8-10 in the world (per head of population)
• The number of athletes in the top 3 in the world (per head of population)
• Athletes receive direct financial support
• Coordinated support programme for elite level athletes (apart from financial support)
• Total gross annual income of athletes
• Gross annual income from sport activities of athletes
• Kind of support services that athletes can make use of (according to athletes)
Stage 2: post-athletic career
• Support for athletes at the end of their careers

Assessment by athletes and coaches
• Satisfaction with support package that athletes receive (according to athletes)
• Satisfaction with the support provided by employer (according to athletes)
• Quality of sport-specific coaches (according to athletes)
• Quality of (para) medical coaches (according to athletes)
• Rating of social and business support (according to athletes)

5.5.1 Key findings
Stage 1: The career of elite athletes

All of the sample nations, apart from Belgium, perform particularly well against the criteria in the competitive and post-career stages of an elite athlete's career. It seems that all nations have invested considerably in this pillar recently. This finding again confirms Oakley and Green's (2001) suggestion that elite sport systems are becoming increasingly homogenous. It is apparent that sports authorities are taking an holistic view of athletes' careers. Talented athletes pursuing their sport are recognised as and treated as employees. Funding for living and sporting costs linked to the minimum wage is in place (although, in the UK, access to funding is subject to 'means-testing') and athletes can also access a range of other lifestyle support services. Generally there is a high degree of satisfaction with financial and other support services from athletes in Flanders, the Netherlands, Canada and Norway. This criterion was not assessed in the other nations. Although the UK athlete survey did not, in this respect, enable direct like-for-like comparisons to be made with the other nations, athletes in the UK were largely satisfied with such services. The only nation which is rated as having a fairly low level of development in this regard is Belgium (both Flanders and Wallonia). Both of these regions of Belgium have a limited number of world ranked athletes, minimal lifestyle support mechanisms (except financial support), and support for athletes at the end of their careers is considered to be poor. To expand these summary points we look at: the number of world ranked athletes in each nation; individual lifestyle support available to athletes; and coaching provided to athletes.

The number of world ranked athletes
The number of world ranked athletes in each nation is an evaluation of the output of an elite sport system rather than the throughput of Pillar 5. It was therefore not weighted as a criterion, but nonetheless it has been evaluated to provide some additional context.

Nations use different criteria for recognising elite athletes and therefore data are difficult to compare on a strictly like for like basis. However, the sample nations provided data on the number of athletes ranked in the top eight and the top three in the world in 2003, which can be linked to population size to compute a standardised measure of world class athletes per million head of population. This analysis is shown in Table 5.2.

Table 5.2: Number of world top 8 and top 3 athletes in the sample nations (2003)

	Number of athletes in the world top 8 (2003)	Athletes /million inhabitants
Canada	227	7.10
Flanders	17	2.83
The Netherlands	461 (343 from Olympic sports and 118 from non-Olympic sports)	28.3 (21.4 if only Olympic sports are included
United Kingdom	240 (mainly Olympic sports)	3.98
Wallonia	8	1.84
	Number of athletes in the world top 3 (2003)	Athletes /million inhabitants
Canada	82	2.54
Italy	119	1.97
United Kingdom	97 (mainly Olympic sports)	1.61
The Netherlands	72 (51 from Olympic sports and 21 from non-Olympic sports)	4.3 (3.1 if only Olympic sports are included)
Flanders	4	0,67
Wallonia	2	0.45

Nb. athletes from Olympic (Summer and/or Winter) sports unless indicated.

Compared with the other nations, the Netherlands appears to have the most athletes per million inhabitants ranked in the world top eight (28.3 per million). This is 15 times more than Wallonia, ten times more than Flanders, seven times more than the UK, and four times more than Canada. This score is partly related to the diverse range of sports (over 60) on which Dutch elite sports policy is focused. Until 2003, federations and athletes in many sports were eligible for subsidies and stipends if they had reached the top eight in the world regardless of whether their sport was football, swimming, athletics, draughts or aero-modelling. In 2003, NOC*NSF tightened up this policy, by reducing the number of 'first category sport disciplines' which are eligible for subsidies and stipends.

Nevertheless, even within Olympic disciplines, the proportion of top 8 athletes in the Netherlands is still much higher than the other nations (three times more than Canada and five times more than the UK). In terms of world top three rankings the number of athletes in the UK and Italy is broadly comparable. The marginally higher number of Canadian top three athletes can mainly be explained by Canada's success in Winter sports and the high priority placed on such sports by the Canadian government. Within the sample nations the Netherlands has the highest number of Olympic medal winning athletes per million inhabitants. An interesting point is the equal pattern of the outflow of athletes in the pyramid in Canada, the UK, and Belgium. On average one in four of the world top eight athletes in these nations are medal winners. Notably, this outflow is smaller in the Netherlands where only one in 6.7 athletes in Olympic disciplines reaches the world top three. This could be a significant finding for Dutch policy, which supports athletes from a relatively broad level of abilities in world terms (the minimum level to qualify for support is the top eight in Europe). One possible explanation for this finding is that supporting many athletes of a lower standard than some of the other sample nations results in the production of more top eight athletes, but the majority of them are unable to win medals. On the other hand, as the Netherlands also has the highest number of top three athletes per inhabitant and the Dutch policy makers may be satisfied with the effectiveness of their investment. Judgements on the efficiency of this investment depend on the priorities made by Dutch government: is it more important to produce contenders (top eight) or medal winners (top three)? Caution must be exercised when interpreting the data as the portfolio of sports included in each nation's sample along with other factors such as squad sizes in team sports can significantly skew the figures.

Individual lifestyle support for athletes

It is difficult to make a comparison of the extent to which direct financial support is received by athletes in each nation. Information on the funding systems of each nation varies significantly; however data have been collated from a wide range of sources to enable some degree of comparability. Athletes receive a monthly salary in most nations. A detailed table is provided in Appendix 7. In the Netherlands a stipend is paid to athletes who are rated in the world top eight and whose yearly income is below the legal minimum income level. In June 2003, there were 452 A-athletes in total and 245 of them received a stipend. In January 2005, these figures were 513 and 289 respectively. 'Stipend' payments range from € 11,474 to € 16,752 per annum. The stipend for A- athletes guarantees athletes the minimum wage so they can train and compete as a full time athlete. In the UK, Athlete Personal Awards are means-tested; athletes can expect to receive awards related to their performance level but subject to the size of their income from other sources, such as sponsorship or employment. Green and Houlihan (2005) concluded that indeed funding for athletes in UK, Canada and Australia was not sufficient to train on a full time basis. Furthermore, athletes with an A-status in the Netherlands can make use of the advice of three counsellors. Both A and B status athletes (1250 in total) are entitled to reimbursement of sport-related costs with an upper limit of € 455 per month for A-athletes and € 137 per month for B-athletes. Since 1992 there has also been a regional network in the Netherlands of 12 Olympic Support centres, where B athletes can receive advice on matters such as technical, medical, social and organisational issues related to their sport.

For Canadian athletes financial assistance is available through the AAP programme, to those already within, or having the potential to reach, the world top 16 in their sport. The amount of assistance ranges from € 632 per month for 'development' athletes to € 1,053 per month for 'senior' athletes. Sometimes support is also provided at provincial level with a good example being Ontario whose government has recently announced a decision to invest extra € 2.5 million in direct financial assistance for athletes.

In the UK, funding eligibility has been based on similar performance levels – top 20 in the world for athletes in individual sports and top 10 in the world for athletes in team sports. In 2003 525 athletes received funding through the World Class Performance Programme (WCPP). On average this was € 15,962 per annum, but the awards ranged from between € 2,908 and € 29,076 depending on the level of achievement and personal factors. UK elite athletes are also supported in several other ways including lifestyle support, sport science and medical support and equipment. High performance athletes from sports that are structured on a "home nation" basis (that is, those with separate English, Welsh, Scottish and Northern Irish governing bodies) are supported via equivalent "national" (rather than UK) programmes. In 2003 there were around 270 athletes supported in this way.

In Norway the athletes receive reimbursements according to their performance in competition. The amount ranges from € 12,000 per annum for A-athletes and € 6,000 for B-athletes, team athletes and athletes under development. According to the elite sports climate survey, 80% of the Norwegian athletes in our survey (summer sports only) receive wages. Norway provides a "24 hour athlete" service where athletes are entitled to medical support, training, nutritional and educational advice at any time of the day. However, all of these facilities are located around Oslo, in the Toppidrettssenteret, a point which is viewed by the Norwegian contributors as a disadvantage.

In Italy, financial support is not managed in a centralised way by a unique national body, rather it is dependent on the specific budget and criteria decided by each national federation. About 400 athletes receive financial support to support their activities twice a year from CONI via the National Governing Bodies. On average this is around € 15,000 per annum plus a retirement fund. In addition to this athletes receive money associated with the winning of Olympic Medals: € 130,000 for a gold medal; € 65,000 for silver and € 40,000 for bronze. For other nations these budgets are not known.

Flemish athletes get paid a 'normal wage' to train; they are in effect given employment contracts as a result of an agreement between the Ministry of Sports and the Ministry of Employment. Generally speaking such athletes should be ranked in the world top 12. The average 'wage' is € 19,294 per annum, and the average amount of reimbursements is € 10,970. Although at the time of writing there were 42 places available, only 36 athletes had reached the requisite performance level enabling them to obtain employment contracts and receive wages. Support of any form in Flanders is limited only to athletes performing at the highest level internationally.

Specific elite athletes in Wallonia also have employment contracts from the Minister of Employment rather than the Minister of Sport. However, further details are not readily available. The total budget for reimbursements paid directly to athletes by the Belgium Olympic Interfederal Committee (BOIC) is also unknown. Flanders and Wallonia are the only sample nations in which athletes can not make use of a co-ordinated support programme, such as sports science, sports medicine and lifestyle support. Generally speaking it can be concluded that a small number of athletes, who receive a normal wage through employment contracts, are well supported; but no support is provided to athletes on a lower level, as is the case in most of the other sample nations.

In the elite sport climate survey, it was found that not all athletes can enjoy the support programmes and financial support mentioned above. Apart from the UK, the level of athletes

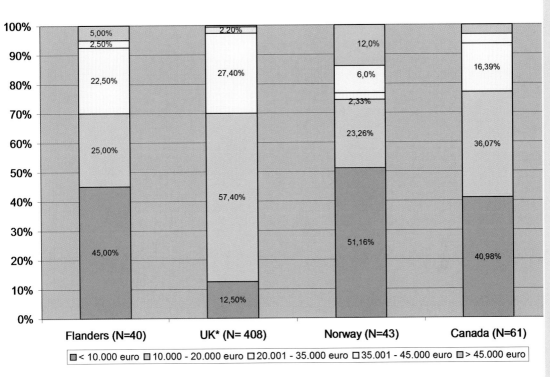

*Note: this figure excludes student athletes, except for the UK

Figure 5.2: Income from sport activities

As can be noticed from Figure 5.2, in the UK the average income reported by athlete respondents was significantly higher than in the other nations: only 12.5% of respondents had an income lower than € 10,000 per year. Caution must be exercised when interpreting these results as the general level of athletes in this research was higher in the UK, Norway and Canada than in Flanders.

In four nations the general support package to athletes was assessed. Dutch athletes were clearly the most satisfied: 72% (a strong majority) evaluated the provision package as satisfactory to good; whereas this view was shared only by minorities in Norway (49%), Canada (44%) and Flanders (40%).

Coaching provided to athletes
An assessment by athletes of the quality of coaching provision was made via the elite sport climate surveys. However, data is not available in the same format for each nation. Whereas the UK data included an evaluation of coaching and other support services using a broad classification of services that was both familiar to UK athletes and consistent with the terminology used in the 1999 survey, Flanders, Norway and the Netherlands rated their coaching and support services across a much wider spectrum of disciplines. Coaching information is not available in any form for Wallonia, Italy or Canada.

In the surveys conducted in Flanders, Norway and the Netherlands, coaching was assessed through specific components of the provision including personal coaching, training from governing bodies, running coaches, conditioning coaches and competition coaches as appropriate. On average, three out of four elite athletes gave a good or satisfactory rating to the level of support received from their various coaches. No significant differences between nations were found. A similar trend can be found for medical and paramedical support. On average 79% of the athletes rated physiotherapists highly and doctors received a 70% positive rating. Athletes seem to be relatively less satisfied with their nutritionists (57%), but fewer athletes made use of these.

Results in the UK appear to be similar to the other sample nations. The majority of UK athletes (a total of 71%) described coaching provision as either good or satisfactory. A further 14% rated the coaching provision as reasonable with only 11% expressing dissatisfaction (the remaining 4% did not answer the question). Medical support in the UK was rated most highly of all the support services, with 74% of athletes rating the service as good (41%) or satisfactory. Across the remaining three nations (Flanders, the Netherlands and Norway) there seemed to be limited use of 'lifestyle' support services specifically lifestyle advisors, business advisors and nutritionists. Where these services were provided, they appear to be rated reasonably highly; however, due to the very low response rates it is not possible to conduct more in depth analysis.

Stage 2: - The post-athletic career
When elite athletes make the choice to engage in sport as a professional career, they often do so to the detriment of a longer term career after their elite sport competition career has ended. Many athletes are insufficiently prepared for life after sports (Anderson & Morris, 2000). Consequently, national sports agencies in various nations have developed programmes to help with this transition both for the benefit of the athletes concerned and their respective sports.

In the Netherlands athletes can seek support for two years after ending their athletic career from NOC*NSF. During these two years, they can have career coaching from an adviser of NOC*NSF. Jointly with the Athletes' Committee, the NOC*NSF also organises symposia for athletes to help them during this time.

In the United Kingdom athletes have access to different services around the nation that can assist them in the development of a new career. The "Performance Lifestyle"service aims to help elite athletes with re-integration after their elite sport career has ended. At the time of writing there were some 40 advisers in the UK who work with athletes individually to achieve this goal.

In Canada athletes can obtain a financial loan of up to a maximum of €3,100 to invest in further education. This loan will be available for as many years as the athlete was 'recognised' as an elite athlete. There is also additional support for athletes who have been 'recognised' for a minimum of three years. Finally workshops through the Canadian Sport Centres are offered to help prepare athletes for the transition into retirement.

In Italy there have been a number of initiatives coordinated by CONI, such as employment through ADECCO (the largest human resources 'solutions' company in the world) and participation in special trainer education processes through NGBs. Other initiatives have also been started by NGBs. Further support programmes, such as pension plans for Italian medal winners were abolished after the Olympic Games of 2000.

Norwegian athletes, after ending their elite sport career, can obtain support from Olympiatoppen and its medical staff on career planning, health and medicine. Also, during their career, athletes receive coaching designed to prepare them for their post-athletic career. As in Italy, athletes can obtain a job through ADECCO.

Wallonia and Flanders are the only nations where there is no specific support for elite athletes who end their sporting career. An athlete's contract of employment terminates when his or her sporting career ends. A private company Randstad Sport aims to support athletes after their career. However, this is a limited provision and only a few athletes make use of it. In Flanders since 2003 young athletes in higher education have received financial support (70%-100% of a normal wage) in order to compensate them for the delay in completing their academic careers. In return for this funding these potential elite athletes are required to spread one year's study over two years. This initiative was set up to motivate athletes to continue their studies and to prepare them for life after sport.

5.6 Pillar 6: Training facilities

Comparative analysis

	CAN	FL	IT	NI	NOR	UK	WAL
Evaluation	○	○	○	○	○	○	NA
Assessment by athletes and coaches	◓	◔	○	◓	◔	◔	●

key
- ◔ policy area very well developed
- ○ good level of development
- ○ moderate level of development
- ◓ fairly low level of development
- ● low level of development
- NA data not available

Selected and available criteria

Evaluation of elite sports facilities and infrastructure
- Existence of national elite sports centre(s) / facilities
- Time spent on travelling for athletes
- Time spent on travelling for coaches
- Database for sports infrastructure and elite sport facilities

Assessment by athletes and coaches
- Quality of training facilities
- Availability of training facilities
- Cooperation of technical staff

5.6.1   Concept and definition

The sixth pillar is concerned with elite sport facilities and infrastructure. These factors were identified as being important by, among others, Oakley and Green (2001b) who identify 'well developed and specific facilities with priority access for elite athletes' as one of ten characteristics commonly found in elite sports development systems. In addition to sport specific training facilities, these institutes also have administrative headquarters and close links with education and sports medicine / science facilities. The components of the network can be centralised; for example the original Australian Institute for Sport which was housed in Canberra; or decentralised, as is the case in the United Kingdom via the English Institute for Sport in the nine regions of England and the home nation equivalents in Scotland, Wales and Northern Ireland.

These elite sport institutes are costly and in many smaller nations less expensive facilities may still be beneficial. Oakley and Green (2001b) showed that large institute networks such as those in France and Australia evolved from large centralised concerns funded by public means to commercial partnerships and from centralised systems to both central and regionally spread networks. Key reasons for this include reducing distances and travelling times for athletes between their homes and their training venues; and reducing 'homesickness' and under performance in young athletes particularly. In this regard a database for sports infrastructure and elite sport facilities may be helpful for a nationally co-ordinated plan to build and renovate sport infrastructure and in order to give priority access to athletes in regional training facilities. In terms of a conducive 'work' environment for elite athletes, athletes themselves value minimising time spent travelling to and from their training venues. Consequently, travelling times for both athletes and coaches is factored in to our definition of what is meant by elite sports facilities and infrastructure.

5.6.2   Key findings

The key point of note is that there is very little discrimination between nations in terms of their scores on Pillar 6. All nations score reasonably highly, a finding that is perhaps not surprising given the increasing homogeneity that has been found in the elite sports development systems of nations adopting a strategic approach to elite sport. Canada scores slightly below the other nations because of the provincial nature of provision and because of the lack of centrally co-ordinated databases monitoring the supply of facilities and supporting infrastructure. Nonetheless, athletes in Canada and Wallonia are relatively dissatisfied with the elite sports facilities in their nations compared with the other sample nations.

The lessons from Australia and France were noted in the UK and a nationwide network of regional high-performance support centres was established. At the time of writing (2006), these were operating under the auspices of the English Sports Institute, the Scottish Sports Institute, the Welsh Institute of Sport and Sports Institute Northern Ireland. By accommodating a variety of sports on individual sites and also providing generic services, the sports institute venues have the potential to be cost effective via economies of scale and non-duplication.

Just like UK, the Canadian system is aimed at delivering services to national governing bodies of sport. Canada has eight elite sport centres spread across the nation in major cities on a regional basis. Close linkages with researchers at universities are being developed and are improving steadily. NGBs in Canada receive funding to pay for the rental costs of sport specific training centres. As these initiatives are only relatively recent, they have not yet been evaluated in the survey, which again shows that time is an important ingredient in elite sport development.

In Italy, national training centres are owned by the NOC (CONI) and are made available to the different national governing bodies of sport, according to their specific needs. For example Tirrenia Center (owned by CONI) is used throughout the year by tennis and baseball, softball and periodically by many other federations. Additional centres are also managed directly by the National Sport Federations. For special purposes however the NGBs often make use of existing private sector facilities. The Italian contributor indicates that the reduction of funding available to CONI has caused major problems in the management and renovation of the elite sports facilities in Italy. In some cases, this has led to a significant reduction in the level of activity at these centres and in extreme cases to their temporary closure.

Norway has a centralised elite sports infrastructure the "Toppidrettssenteret" in Oslo, which includes a sport science department that works in close co-operation with universities. In the Netherlands, there is the National Centre for Sports at Papendal, managed by the NOC*NSF. Papendal includes among other things an athletics track, indoor sports facilities, a hotel and a conference hall. Furthermore, the Netherlands has two other national sport centres: the KNVB Sports Centre in Zeist (Utrecht) and the Euregional Sport and Congress centre in Sittard.

The Flemish Sports administration, Bloso owns two elite sports facilities (the elite sports hall in Ghent and Bloso-centre Netepark in Herentals) for several subsidised elite sports. These are modern facilities and include hotel provision for athletes. However, there is no direct link with sports medicine / science or with the elite sport and study systems in Flanders. Bloso owns 11 other centres for sport, aimed primarily at recreational sport, but where elite athletes are offered priority access and other advantages. The policy survey research revealed that these extra facilities had yet to reach a globally competitive standard. The situation in Wallonia is comparable. Adeps owns sport centres at which elite athletes can train in good conditions and have priority access.

Through this information we can confirm Oakley and Green's (2001b) finding that there is an increasing tendency to develop similar institute networks but with local variations shaped by the specific traditions and patterns of government involvement in sport. Although the elite sports infrastructure is clearly present in a number of nations, its availability for elite athletes is not always evident. For instance, elite swimmers in many nations are often only able to train early in the morning or late in the evening i.e. outside of peak mass participation times.

To verify whether elite sports facilities actually meet the needs of athletes, coaches and co-ordinators, they were evaluated by the respondents in the elite sports climate survey. In terms of competition and training facilities, there was relatively little variation in the opinions of the respondents, with only Canada and Wallonia yielding results that are significantly more negative than the international group: scarcely 21% of the Canadian and 22% of the Walloon respondents considered training facilities to be satisfactory. Competition facilities in these two nations were rated even lower.

The elite athletes in the United Kingdom were the most satisfied with an 80% approval rating, followed by Norway, with 67%. In Flanders and the Netherlands the majority of respondents were satisfied with their training facilities (56% and 54% respectively). The views of coaches in this respect were similar to those of athletes. The findings relating to the availability of training facilities were closely correlated with the overall ratings of the quality of training facilities. Norway had the highest level of satisfaction (83%), closely followed by UK (76%).

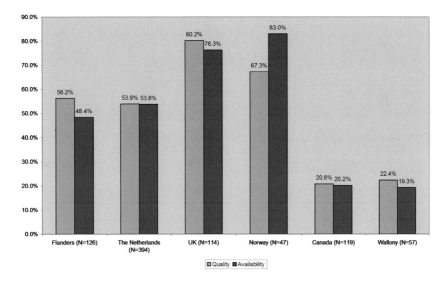

Figure 5.3: The proportion of athletes rating quality and availability of training facilities satisfactory/good

The same pattern emerges when we look at the number of hours per week that athletes in each nation spend travelling to and from their training facilities. In each of the five nations for which data is available (i.e. excluding Italy and Wallonia), 80% of the athletes spent less than 10.5 hours per week travelling and for 50% of respondents weekly travelling times were less than 5.5 hours.

In short, the supply of elite sport training facilities has developed in a manner which takes into account the needs and comfort of elite athletes. It is no longer good practice to provide facilities on a supply-led basis. When considering the needs of athletes from an holistic perspective, considerations such as proximity to family and friends as well as minimising travelling times and the potential for homesickness are important factors. Consequently, the current generation of elite sports facilities and supporting infrastructure tend to be provided on a decentralised and demand-led basis. The provision of facilities for elite sport is very visible. Therefore, nations that are relative newcomers to the world of strategic elite sports development systems can see and learn from the experiences of the 'early adopters'.

CHAPTER 5

5.7 Pillar 7:
Coaching provision and coach development

Comparative analysis

	CAN	FL	IT	NI	NOR	UK	WAL
Evaluation	NA	◉	○	○	NA	○	◉
Assessment by coaches	NA	○	◉	○	NA	NA	●

key		
	○	policy area very well developed
	○	good level of development
	○	moderate level of development
	◉	fairly low level of development
	●	low level of development
	NA	data not available

NB: Canada and Norway supplied data on relatively few criteria and did not participate in the elite sport climate survey
NB: (*) Low response rates from coaches in the UK (8%) and Wallonia (20%)

Selected and available criteria

Number and level of coaches
- Number of qualified coaches
- Existence of coaches database
- Level reached by coach in his/her own career as an athlete
- Proportion of coaches who have undertaken governing body training (qualification)
- Proportion of coaches who have undertaken governing body refresher training

Coach development system
- Existence within coach education system of elite coach qualification
- Services and resources supporting the continuous professional development of coaches

Individual circumstances
- Gross annual income of coaches (i.e. from coaching activities)
- Availability of reimbursements from governing bodies and clubs
- Proportion of coaches with written contracts of employment

Assessment by coaches

Quality of career prospects for elite coaches
Extent to which coaching (at an elite level) is recognized as a career
Quality of
- governing body coach development programmes
- individual training courses

Sufficiency of training opportunities (courses) for elite coaches
Extent to which employers take account of the training needs of elite coaches
Extent to which coaches are able to give enough extra attention to upcoming talents

5.7.1   Concepts and definitions

In Chapter 3 of this book, we outlined a number of inter-nation variations in the size and structure of the athlete and coach samples that participated in our various elite sport climate surveys. In considering our assessment of coaching provision and coach development, four particular features should be noted. First, neither Norway nor Canada carried out a survey of coaches as part of their elite sports climate survey. We therefore have insufficient data on these two nations to include them in our evaluation. Second, the UK's coach survey was considerably different to those carried out in Flanders, the Netherlands and Wallonia. This was because UK Sport (which commissioned the research) required the coach questionnaire to cover a similar set of issues to that included in the UK athlete survey, with the result that several areas of inquiry were not covered in the UK version. Third, there were very low response rates in the UK (8%) and in Wallonia (20%). Fourth, whereas the Netherlands, United Kingdom and Wallonia sought to involve only coaches who work, or have worked, with elite athletes, this turned out not to be the case in Flanders and Italy, where only around 70% of the coaches surveyed operated at this level. The others are youth coaches developing promising youngsters. However, in depth analysis on the data showed that in these two nations almost no significant differences could be found in the results between coaches working with established elite athletes and coaches working with elite youth athletes.

Our assessment is divided into three main areas – the number and level of coaches in each nation; coach development provision; and coaches' individual living circumstances.

5.7.2   Key findings

Number and level of coaches
In terms of the number of qualified coaches, the indications are that the Netherlands and Canada are the best-provided nations, with ratios of around nine coaches per 1000 population each. Figures for Flanders suggest a ratio of 5:1000, and for Italy and the UK only 3:1000. Despite a paucity of information in other respects, we did establish that coaching provision in Canada is proportionately similar to the Netherlands. Canada's favourable performance in this respect may not be unrelated to the fact that it is the only one of the sample nations to maintain a national database of practising coaches at all levels: it could be that nations that do not have such a resource tend to underestimate numbers. Furthermore, we believe that Canada and Italy are the only sample nations in which people are universally required to have a coaching qualification in order to coach in sports clubs. In Italy this requirement is restricted to the competitive sport system and skiing instruction.

At least 85% of elite coach respondents from Italy, Flanders and Wallonia indicated that they were fully qualified (i.e. that they had completed their governing body's coach training course). The proportion of Dutch elite coaches who were fully qualified was somewhat lower, at 66%. Another indicator of coaching levels was the proportion of elite coaches who had competed at an international level in their own career as an athlete. Here the figures ranged from 60% of Dutch coaches to 36% of Flemish coaches (in the case of Flanders, this calculation was made after filtering out youth coaches from the sample). Amongst the small number of elite UK coaches who responded to the survey, 94% had competed at an international level.

Coach development provision

In terms of career development opportunities for coaches, our view is that amongst participating nations, the UK and Canada are currently making the greatest provision. The UK operates a five-level flexible coaching certificate, of which levels 4 and 5 apply to elite coaches. In 2004 a new elite coach acceleration programme for individuals nominated by NGBs as their 'rising stars of coaching' was also founded and plans were announced to appoint 45 new Coach Development Officers to support national governing bodies and sub-regional "sports partnerships" in accessing high-quality coach education and continuous professional development opportunities. In Canada, the National Coaching Certificate Programme also covers the range of coaching experience and ability. Formerly structured around five levels in either theory, technical or practical, it is now based around five competencies and divided into community sport, competition or instruction.

The Netherlands again also rated highly in our assessment. The 'Master Coach in Sport' programme aims to develop a personal education plan for elite coaches who work with A or B status athletes. All coaches on this one-year programme must have a Physical Education degree and / or the highest NGB coaching qualification. Furthermore, in the Netherlands, sport-technical consultants have been appointed by NOC*NSF to assist coaches. At the sub-elite level however, there is no national coordination of coach education in terms of the standard and content of courses in different sports.

In Italy the level IV coach qualification is organised by the NOC, through the Scuola dello sport, in cooperation with the NGBs. As in the Netherlands, this is a one-year programme targeting elite coaches to improve their skills and knowledge, expressly dedicated to top athletes and team training and management.

We considered that the least well developed approach to coach development was in Belgium. In Flanders and Wallonia, the Flemish Training School (VTS) and the "École de moniteurs et d'entraîneurs" coordinate respectively a three or four level coach education programme. Although these coach education systems are well developed and positively assessed by coaches, there is no elite training course or official certificate associated with this programme. These issues are flagged as a major weakness in the sports climate of these nations. Services aimed at promoting the development of coaches at the highest level are virtually non-existent, except when the federation takes initiatives itself. It should be noted that the new policy framework for Flanders calls for the organization of continued professional development for elite coaches, and a review of the need for an elite coaches' diploma by the year 2009 (Anciaux, 2004).

Another important aspect of coach development services is the opportunity for information exchange. We identified that most participating nations provide some form of coaching forum or discussion group and/or a dedicated publication or website platform. In Flanders and Wallonia, however, this occurs only when the federations themselves lead the process.

Systems for developing elite coaches were evaluated by the coaches. On average, about half of the coaches in each nation were satisfied with the level of the continuing education and coach training. An exception was Wallonia, where a large number of respondents (62%) rated such courses as poor or insufficient (n=13). Also in Italy the views were less positive where 50% of respondents rated the general training as poor or insufficient (n=31).

Individual living circumstances

Among our sample nations, only in the UK was there any evidence that direct financial support has been provided to coaches. But even here, this support has been confined to the personal coaches of elite athletes (that is, coaches not directly employed by national governing bodies) in the run-up to, and at, major events.

In terms of coaches' gross annual income, UK coaches clearly emerge as the best paid, with one third of coach respondents indicating that they earn more than € 50,000 annually from their sport. (Again, we need to treat these data with caution because of the low response rate amongst UK elite coaches.) Dutch coaches reported the next highest levels of income, with around 40% (n=16) indicating that they earn over € 25,000 per annum.

In Flanders almost 60% of coaches earn less than € 10,000 per year from their coaching activities and only 3% said they earn more than € 50,000 per year. It is in recognition of these sorts of circumstances that the new policy plan for Flanders (2005-2009) will create a pool of 42 full-time domestic or foreign coaches who will be offered an employment contract to work with elite athletes.

Among the six nations, only one nation currently has a statute for coaches. In the Netherlands, the Federation Dutch Trade Union (FNV), which is the largest trade union with 1.2 million members, has a division for sport (FNV Sport), that represents all employees and trainers who work in sports. Until 2005, there was also the National Federation for Workers in Sport, whose mission was to promote the expertise of the trainer/coach and the professionalisation of the coaching profession. This organisation ceased to exist in 2005 and merged with NL-Coach, with Joop Alberda (coach of the gold winning volleyball team in 1996 and technical manager of the Dutch Olympic team in 1998, 2000, 2002 and 2004) as its initiator and current president. We already know that, in many nations, it is difficult to operate as a full time coach (Green and Houlihan, 2005). Potentially high quality coaches are often lost to coaching because they are forced to seek employment in other areas (Clumpner 1994). In Flanders, the Netherlands and Wallonia, over two thirds of coach respondents indicated that they were unable to devote sufficient time to the talented, up-and-coming athletes with whom they were involved. Italian coaches were slightly more positive in this respect even though, unlike in Flanders and the Netherlands, they appeared to receive little recognition from their employers about the demands of being an elite coach. These issues were not examined in the UK's coach survey. Against this background, it is not surprising that coaches in Italy, Flanders, the Netherlands and Wallonia all expressed dissatisfaction about the recognition of their job and their career prospects.

In conclusion it appears that among our sample nations, the Netherlands and the UK rate most highly in their efforts to professionalise the coaching industry and to recognise and support individual coaches, including those operating at the elite level. Problems appear to persist in Flanders and Wallonia. Although our Policy surveys provide some evidence of a positive environment for coaching in Norway and Canada, the fact that Norwegian and Canadian coaches did not participate in the elite sports climate survey means that we cannot draw any meaningful conclusions about these two nations.

5.8 Pillar 8: International competition

Comparative analysis

	CAN	FL	IT	NI	NOR	UK	WAL
Evaluation: organisation of international events	○	○	○	◉	○	◔	◉
Assessment by athletes and coaches (organisation of international elite sport events)	◔	●	○	◔	◔	◔	●
Assessment by athletes and coaches (participation in international competition)	○	○	○	○	◔	○	○

key
- ◔ policy area very well developed
- ○ good level of development
- ○ moderate level of development
- ◉ fairly low level of development
- ● low level of development
- NA data not available

Selected and available criteria
- Availability of funding for the bidding for, and the staging of, major international sports events
- Central coordination of such funding
- Provision to governing bodies of assistance with, and advice on, the organisation of major international sports events

Assessment by athletes and coaches
- Satisfaction with the number of major international sports events organised in own nation
- Satisfaction with the amount of suitable international competition in which athletes can take part

5.8.1   Concept and definition

Competition, both at national and international level, is an important factor in the development of athletes (Crespo, Miley & Couraud, 2001; Green & Houlihan, 2005; Oakley & Green, 2001b). It allows athletes to measure themselves against rivals, individually or as a team. Competition opportunities at national level should be analysed at a sport-specific level, as conducted by Green and Houlihan (2005) in swimming, athletics and yachting in the UK, Canada and Australia. They suggest that high quality, regular domestic competitions and structures below the elite level are important for talented athletes to compete at the highest level and to offset the cost of travelling further abroad. These characteristics are even more important in large nations.

International competition opportunities can be enhanced for athletes when major sports are organised in the own nation, as has been shown in many studies on the Olympic Games (Bernard and Busse, 2000; Clarke, 2002; Johnson and Ali, 2002; Kuper and Sterken, 2003). Our analysis of pillar 8 is confined simply to three key areas: firstly, the extent to which there is a national policy and support system for the organization of major international sports events in each nation; secondly, the views of athletes, coaches and performance directors on the sufficiency of major events held in their nation; and thirdly, the satisfaction of athletes and coaches with their opportunities to participate in international competitions.

5.8.2   Key findings

The market for major international sports events is a global one in which the holders of property rights (normally international federations) seek to maximize the financial benefit to themselves from host promoters. Although the provision of such events is, therefore, generally not under the control of national governing bodies, the co-ordinated development of an events "culture" can and often does take place at national level.

In the United Kingdom and the Netherlands the organisation of international events is coordinated nationally and there is a long-term event strategy. This in turn explains the higher scores of these two nations on this pillar. Our assessment is that the UK's approach is the most advanced of the sample nations. A key part of UK Sport's Major Events Strategy, the UK World Class Events Programme (WCEP) provides financial resources and expertise to assist governing bodies and cities looking to bid for and stage major events. The WCEP is supported by a comprehensive information service and has resulted in a portfolio of good practice which UK Sport shares with partner organisations, notably at its annual World Class Events Conference. In the Netherlands, co-ordinating responsibility is held by the Information Centre for Elite Sport Competitions (ICESC). This centre, established in 2002 by NOC*NSF, implements a long term plan for all elite sporting competitions that take place in the Netherlands. However, some NGBs pursue their own interests independently of ICESC. Canada has followed the example set by the UK and the Netherlands by recently developing its own national strategy for hosting major sports events. In Flanders the organisation and funding of events is coordinated by the recently established steering group for elite sport. However, currently there is no annual or long-term planning cycle. In Italy, Norway and Wallonia there is no co-ordination of funding or support for major sports events.

Although we were unable to establish detailed figures for each nation, we believe that governments in all the sample nations provide some level of funding for the bidding for and / or the staging of major sports events. We are aware that UK Sport invests around €2.2million per year in the WCEP.

Looking at the views of athletes, coaches and performance directors in the round, we found almost universal dissatisfaction with the sufficiency of suitable international competitions that take place in respondents' own nations. Only amongst Italian coaches (53%) and Flemish co-ordinators (50%) did at least half of respondents express the view that a sufficient number of events was available. Given the nature of the events "market" as discussed above, it is difficult to gauge the legitimacy of these views. However, given the significant efforts and investment made by the UK in trying to attract major events to its shores, the fact that over 60% of its athletes indicated dissatisfaction with the number of suitable events in which they are able to take part in the UK [this was a slightly different question to that asked elsewhere] may suggest that athlete respondents in our survey exhibited unrealistic expectations in this respect. Of course, London had not yet won its bid for the 2012 Olympics when the survey took place; were the survey to be run again, it is possible that a rather different picture might emerge in this respect.

We also asked elite sport climate survey respondents about the sufficiency of international competitions in which athletes can take part – wherever those events might be held. In this case, athletes in Norway and the Netherlands were the most positive, with 67% and 61% of Norwegian and Dutch athletes respectively saying that they were satisfied with the opportunities available. In the case of UK athletes who answered a slightly different question, 78% expressed a positive view about the sufficiency of suitable competitive events in which they can take part overseas. It is difficult to draw firm conclusions from these data. On the one hand, the findings might to some extent reflect athletes' satisfaction with the competition programmes and support provided by their governing body; on the other, they might be explained simply by the differences in the international competition structures of different sports.

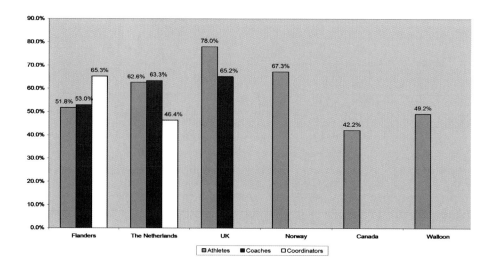

Figure 5.4: Satisfaction on Participation in international competitions

5.9   Pillar 9:
Scientific research

Comparative analysis

	CAN	FL	IT	NI	NOR	UK	WAL
Evaluation	○	◉	○	○	○	◉	●
Assessment			no assessment available				

key

⬭	policy area very well developed
○	good level of development
○	moderate level of development
⬬	fairly low level of development
●	low level of development
NA	data not available

Selected and available criteria

Scientific research
- Nations have a national research centre
- National co-ordination: there is a network of scientific information and communication directed towards coaches / governing bodies
- Co-operation with universities / research centres is co-ordinated at national level
- Specific subsidies for scientific research in elite sport are provided
- Coaches receive scientific information from their governing body

5.9.1 Concept and definition

The ninth pillar is concerned with the "scientific backdrop" to elite sport, in connection with which we sought to examine the extent to which nations take a coordinated approach to the organisation and dissemination of research and scientific information. These factors were indirectly referred to by Oakley and Green (2001b) when they identified as one of ten characteristics commonly found in elite sports development systems, the "provision of sports services to create a culture of excellence in which all members of the team (athletes, coaches, managers and scientists) can interact." Developments in sports science was also one of the four key points made in the analysis by Green and Houlihan (2005).

5.9.2 Key findings

In our assessment, Norway appears to have the most coherent approach to scientific research amongst our sample nations. This slightly higher score than other nations is largely explained by the relatively high level of funding devoted to research in Norway. There has been a national research programme for sport in Norway since 1998 that provides the opportunity for information exchange between sports, and is a funding source for both national governing bodies of sport and universities. However, this programme will end in 2007. There is good co-operation between Olympiatoppen and its researchers with the Norwegian School of Sport Sciences, the University of Trondheim and the University of Oslo.

The other sample nations generally differ only slightly in the evaluation of pillar 9. Italy, is the only nation with a National Olympic Institute (NOI). Since the 1970s the NOI has housed a sports-specific scientific institute (Instituto dello Sport) providing psychological, medical and biomechanical support for athletes. Product knowledge has traditionally been seen as a strength in Italy. In the 1980s and 1990s sport research in Italy was recognised as among the most advanced in the world. Recently, however, CONI has reduced the funding made available for scientific research to support elite sport.

Although there is no dedicated research centre in the Netherlands, considerable attention is paid nationally to the co-ordination, collection and dissemination of scientific research and information about elite sport. This is led by the Elite Sports Expert Centre (TEC), which was established by NOC*NSF, and acts as a focal point for coaches and federations looking to commission or undertake applied research. Information is available online via TECnet or Bondnet (for federations), and NOC*NSF regularly publishes research-related reports and articles.

The dissemination of information through the Sport Information Resource Centre (SIRC) in Canada is the nearest parallel to the Dutch situation, although this database producer is a global concern and its output is not only for Canadian coaches or NSOs. Its subscribers range from universities, libraries and hospitals to coaches, athletes, professors and medical practitioners. SIRC's best-known product is its extended database of scientific research, Sport Discus. The National Coaching Institutes (NCIs) across Canada are subscribers to SPORTDiscus, thereby enabling athletes and coaches to gain access to various sport-related documentation (Sport Canada, 2006).

In the UK, Wallonia and Flanders, there is again no national research centre or centralised online dissemination system. This explains the fairly low level of development scores given to these nations. In the UK, the British Association of Sport & Exercise Sciences (BASES) nevertheless seeks to promote fundamental and applied research in the sport and exercise sciences and to disseminate knowledge. In addition, one of the roles of UK Sport is to provide a link between sports and technical experts. Coaches and athletes from the sports concerned are usually closely involved.

Most nations in our sample provide some level of funding for scientific research in elite sport. In the United Kingdom, UK Sport has invested around € 350,000 per year in sport-specific research and development projects, and federations (since 2004, this figure has risen to around € 1 million) can also obtain funding for scientific research via the World Class Performance Programme. In Norway the amount is limited to € 500,000 specifically for elite sport and which is mostly used for equipment research.

None of the nations has a nationally co-ordinated programme of co-operation with universities and higher education establishments for the purpose of scientific research. The difficulty of engaging academic institutions in applied research is a universal and long-standing problem. In many nations, university funded research is often inadequate for the type of investigation needed for elite sport. This point is consistent with Green and Houlihan's (2005) study of Australian swimming. A number of nations are nevertheless taking steps to bridge this gap. In Flanders, universities are represented in the coach education system (i.e. the Flemish training school) and in 'think tanks' in individual sports. Furthermore, the Ministry provides around €300,000 a year for sport research, to be divided among the three universities in Flanders with a department for physical education. In Italy, CONI and the Ministry of Education recently established a joint committee to improve coordination. In Canada, consideration is being given to an applied science programme with universities and colleges at both the federal level and within individual sports. Nonetheless, only 29% of the Flemish coaches received scientific information from their governing body. In Wallonia this score was lower (24%; n = 17) and the highest score was found in the UK where 87% (n = 23) of the coaches received scientific information from their governing body.

Having completed the review of the nine pillars in isolation, in Chapter 6 we bring the results together to illustrate the performance of each nation against all of the pillars on a nation by nation basis. Using the data from Chapter 4 on performance and Chapter 5 on the nine pillars, we then explore potential links between the input and throughput phases and the output phase.

Chapter 6:
Key Findings

6.1   The global context

Competition for success in elite sport is increasing. More nations are adopting strategic approaches towards the development of elite athletes and as a result an increasing number of nations have developed genuine medal winning capability. As the supply of success, that is, the number of events and medals that can be contested is relatively fixed, and demand for success is increasing, the 'market' adjusts by raising the price of success. The price of success is the investment in revenue and capital required to produce success. We endorse the opinions of other authors who describe this situation as a 'global sporting arms race'.

Our research supports the view that the resource implication of this so-called global sporting arms race is considerable. The policy surveys reveal a remarkable acceleration in the funding for sport (including elite sport) in the Athens Olympiad among the sample nations as shown in Figure 6.1.

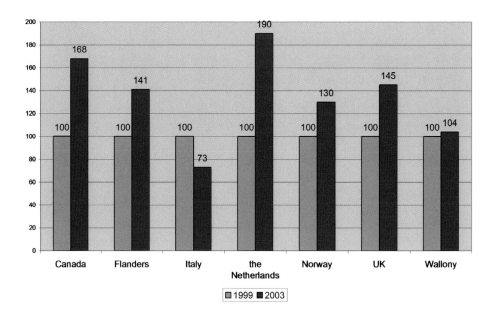

Figure 6.1: Change in expenditure on elite sport from 1999 – 2003

Expenditure on sport increased considerably in the four years 1999-2003 in four of the six sample nations. Italy was the only exception in this regard, with a reduction in expenditure of 27% caused by falling sport gambling receipts. Expenditures in elite sport also more than doubled in the UK (226%) and Flanders (215%) and increased considerably in Wallonia (182%) and the Netherlands (154%).

We found amongst the sample nations that governments and national sports agencies were fully committed to enhancing and supporting their respective elite sport systems and that the growth in funding for elite sport specifically was greater than the funding for sport generally. Interestingly, as can be seen from Figure 6.2 no nation in the sample improved its market share in the summer Olympic Games of Athens 2004 compared with Sydney 2000 despite the near universal increase in funding for sport generally.

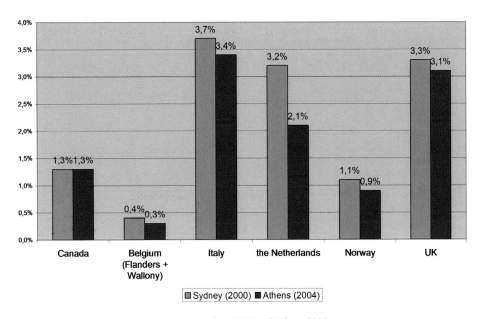

Figure 6.2: Change in market share between Sydney 2000 and Athens 2004

Figure 6.2 illustrates that none of the sample nations improved its market share from Sydney to Athens and that Canada was the only nation which maintained its performance (1.3% on both occasions) during the period. This finding suggests that as nations strive for success there are diminishing returns on investment such that it is necessary to continue investing in elite sport simply to maintain existing performance levels. This is a salutary lesson for the United Kingdom as it bids to improve from 10th place in Sydney and Athens to 4th place in 2012 when London will host the Olympic Games. From the sample nations alone, competition will be particularly stiff from the Netherlands as the Dutch government expressed its support in 2005 to the sports sector "to ensure the Netherlands ranks among the top ten nations in the international sports world".

In most sample nations there appears to be a funding model based on a combination of Exchequer (on balance sheet) and Lottery (off balance sheet) funding. In nations where Lottery funding is relatively high, state funding tends to be relatively low and vice versa. Lottery proceeds tend to be volatile and when proceeds fall, the elite sport community will appeal to government for additional state support. Italy is a good example of a nation where a fall in Lottery funding has led to a previously indifferent state guaranteeing a minimum level of funding for sport via substantially increased Exchequer funding.

6.2 Performance in sport

Table 6.1 demonstrates considerable variation in the relative performance of the sample nations in international sport. This variation is a function of the portfolio of sports and events included in the analysis. When a diverse portfolio of 60 sports is analysed, the UK emerges as the most successful sporting nation in the sample largely because of the breadth of sports in which it takes part including non-Olympic and professional sports.

Table 6.1: Relative performance of sample nations in international sport

Nation	Athens 2004	WSI* 60 Sports 2004	All Olympic Sports 2004	Torino 2006
Italy	1st	3rd	2nd	2nd
United Kingdom	2nd	1st	4th	5th
Netherlands	3rd	5th	5th	4th
Canada	4th	2nd	1st	1st
Norway	5th	4th	3rd	3rd
Belgium	6th	6th	6th	6th

*WSI = UK Sport World Sporting Index

When the focus is narrowed down to Olympic sports only, the UK performs relatively poorly because its weak performance in Winter Olympic sports dilutes its success in Summer Olympic sports. Canada emerges as the top nation on the same basis – i.e. because of its strength in Winter Olympic sports. If the portfolio of sports is narrowed down again - to Summer Olympic sports only - then Italy is the most successful nation in the sample and has been so for much of the modern era (post 1948). In Summer Olympic terms, Canada's is ranked 4th among the sample nations, which is slightly below expectation in terms of population and wealth (3rd). These findings suggest that Canada has different sporting priorities to the UK and Italy and seems to be pursuing a strategy of 'priority' rather than 'diversity', where the priority is on Winter Olympic sports.

The Netherlands was ranked 3rd of the sample nations in Athens 2004 but slightly lower in all other indices. On the basis of resources available, (population and GDP), this is a better than expected level of achievement, which in turn suggests a successful focus on Summer Olympic sports. In Winter Olympic sports the Netherlands performs in line with expectations. However, for a nation which explicitly takes a 'diversity' rather than 'priority' approach to performance, it might be argued that a sample nation ranking of 5th in the UK Sport World Sporting Index is somewhat disappointing. The counter to this argument is that some of the activities which the Netherlands supported until 2003, such as korfball, chess, bridge and aero model flying, are not included in the UK Sport World Sporting Index. Other sports included in the index, such as cricket, are not very popular in the Netherlands. In this regard the performance of the Netherlands in what it might consider to be 'international sport' is therefore perhaps understated.

Norway's performance can be summarised as a scaled-down version of Canada. Norway clearly prioritises Winter Olympic sports and is successful in winning medals in them. Concentrated success in a narrow portfolio of sports enables Norway to have high rankings in other indices.

Although its performance in the summer Olympics is slightly better than might be expected (5th among the sample nations rather than 6th), it is still Norway's lowest ranking in Table 6.1.

Belgium is consistently ranked 6th in Table 6.1. On the basis of resources available, it might be expected that Belgium would be more successful than Norway, but this is not the case. The analysis does not take account of Norway's prioritisation of winter sports and the existence of natural resources that enable it to do so.

The key point arising from the analysis of sporting performance is that a nation's performance in international sport is not an absolute. Before a cross-national assessment of performance can be made, due consideration needs to be given to how the notion of 'performance' is to be measured. Broad measures such as the UK Sport World Sporting Index favour nations such as the UK which have traditions in a wide range of Olympic and non-Olympic sports. When narrowing the focus down to Olympic sports we find that some nations perform better in summer Olympic sports, some perform better in winter Olympic sports and some perform well in both. Thus performance in international sport is a function of how 'international sport' is defined.

In the following section we examine the sample nations' performance against the criteria found in each of the nine pillars discussed in Chapter 5 to see if there is any link between performance against these factors and any of the sporting performance indices outlined in Table 6.1.

6.3   Performance against the nine pillars

In this section we summarise the overall performance of each nation against the nine pillars using the series of colour coded signals shown in Table 6.2 below.

Table 6.2: The key to pillar rating charts

○	Policy area very well developed
○	Good level of development
○	Moderate level of development
●	Limited development
●	Little or no development

N.B. Pillars 1 (Financial Inputs) & 2 (Integrated Approach to Policy Development) use a slightly different formulation in line with the particular area of policy they describe

The following ratings provide an indication of the extent to which each policy area has been developed in each sample nation. The findings are set out in Table 6.3. It should be noted that these ratings are, in effect, a relative assessment of the elite sport systems of this particular group of nations. Therefore if more nations were to be added to the sample, it is possible that we might need to adjust our ratings to take account of wider variations in practice – whether good or less good. Table 6.4 summarises the way in which athletes, coaches and performance directors rate the quality of, or their satisfaction with, the same areas of policy: in effect, these views can be thought of as providing a commentary on the findings shown in Table 6.3.

Table 6.3: SPLISS EVALUATION OF POLICY FACTORS
(Nations ordered by assessed ranking in summer Olympic sports)

	ITA	UK	NED	CAN	NOR	FLA	WAL
1(a) Financial support: National expenditure on sport	○	○	○	◐	◐	◐	◐
1(b) Financial support: National governing bodies	○	◐	○	◐	●	●	●
2. Integrated approach to policy development	○	○	○	○	◐	○	○
3. Participation in sport	◐	○	○	NA	○	○	○
4. Talent identification & development system	●	◐	◐	◐	○	○	◐
5. Athletic and post career support	○	◐	○	○	○	◐	◐
6. Training facilities	○	○	○	○	○	○	NA
7. Coaching provision and coach development	○	◐	○	NA	NA	◐	◐
8. International competition (organisation events)	○	◐	◐	○	○	○	◐
9. Scientific research	○	◐	○	○	○	◐	●

Table 6.4: ASSESSMENT BY ATHLETES AND COACHES
(Nations ordered by assessed ranking in summer Olympic sport)

	ITA	UK	NED	CAN	NOR	FLA	WAL
1. Financial support (a) National expenditure on sport							
1. (b) Financial support for national governing bodies							
2. Integrated approach to policy development	◐	NA	○	NA	○	◐	NA
3. Participation in sport							
4. Talent identification & development system	○	NA	○	NA	○	◐	●
5. Athletic and post career support	NA	NA	◐	○	○	○	NA
6. Training facilities	○	◐	◐	◐	◐	◐	●
7. Coaching provision and coach development	◐	NA	○	NA	NA	○	●
8. International competition (a) organisation of international events	○	◐	◐	◐	◐	●	●
8. (b) participation in international events	○	○	○	○	◐	○	○
9. Scientific research							

Overall, there are relatively few areas in which there are significant variations between the sample nations. The absence of such discrimination lends weight to the argument about the largely homogenous approach that different nations appear to be taking to the development of their elite sport systems. We evaluated seven 'nations' (two in Belgium) across nine pillars which in turn were made up of more then 100 criteria. Thus there were 63 (7 x 9) summary ratings made and only four of these were 'Not Available.

When looking at athletes and coaches to validate and elaborate on the findings from the policy surveys we find two key points. First, there are considerably more 'Not Available answers in Table 6.4 than in Table 6.3 which reflects how difficult it was to obtain responses from certain sample groups as discussed in Chapter 3. Second, where rating of responses is possible there is some degree of consistency between the policy surveys and the views of athletes and coaches. The most noticeable difference is found in Pillar 8 (International Competition) where athletes and coaches were asked whether they felt that sufficient international events were held in their nation. Our view is that, in this instance, athletes and coaches have higher expectations than it is realistically possible to deliver. Like sporting success there is also a global market for hosting major sports events and thus it is inevitable that any given nation will be able to host only a limited number of major sports events over a given period.

However, despite the limitations of the research it is possible in broad terms to examine the relative strengths and weaknesses of each nation's policy factors. We have conducted this analysis by plotting the rankings for each nation on each factor against the sample averages using 'radar' graphs. The radar graph for the UK is shown below in Figure 6.3

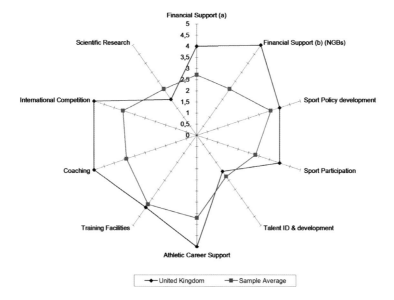

Figure 6.3: Radar graph for the UK

In Figure 6.3 it can be seen that the UK achieves the maximum score of '5' (policy area very well developed) for four of the ten policy factors. Furthermore, with the exception of slightly below average scores for talent identification and development and for scientific research, the UK meets or exceeds the sample average for eight of the ten policy factors. Where the UK appears to have its greatest advantage is in Pillar 1, support to National governing bodies for which the gap between its score and the sample averages is +2.4. This finding suggests that elite sport in the UK is funded considerably better than in the other sample nations. Cross referencing with Table 6.3 confirms that the UK is the nation with the best combined score for Pillars 1a and 1b.

If there is a link between the efficacy of policy factors and performance in elite sport, it would be reasonable to expect the UK to be a successful sporting nation. This notion will be tested more thoroughly in the conclusions.

As a contrast to the UK position, Figure 6.4 illustrates the performance of Flanders against the sample averages using the same radar style graph used for the UK above.

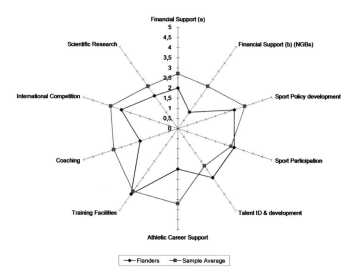

Figure 6.4: Radar graph for Flanders

Flanders appears to have a relative strength in Pillar 4 (talent identification and development) compared with the sample average. Against the other nine factors Flanders is equal to the sample average for Pillar 3 (participation in sport) and Pillar 6 (training facilities) and below the sample average for the seven other factors.

The magnitude of the gaps between the scores for Flanders and the sample average are greatest in financial support for governing bodies (-1.6), athletic career support (-1.7) and coaching (-1.4). In terms of Flanders narrowing the gap between itself and the other sample nations, the three policy areas with the greatest gap between the region's score and the sample average should be viewed as priority areas for investment.

Radar graphs based on the scores in Table 6.3 for the other nations in the sample are shown in Appendix 8. We now conclude the report by looking at the key findings and offering some possible explanations.

6.4 Key conclusions

The relationship between policy and performance

The key question concerning elite sport development posed at the beginning of this book was whether there is a relationship between the evaluation of each pillar (the inputs and the throughputs) and the output (international performances). We need to preface our conclusions by re-stating that our assessment of the relative ranking of the sample nations varies considerably according to the index used to define success (see Table 6.1). Any attempt to identify a relationship between the quality of elite sport systems and nations' performance in international sport is therefore going to be problematic.

The two nations whose performance is easiest to understand are Italy and Belgium. Italy performs consistently well across the range of indices we have used to measure success, while Belgium (represented jointly by Flanders and Wallonia) performs consistently poorly. However, although the policy scores for Belgium are reflective of its performance standing (Flanders and Wallonia achieve only one "good level of development" rating between them[8]), the scores for Italy do not do justice to a successful sporting nation for all pillars. In Italy, no policy area achieves a top rating and development is assessed as no higher than "moderate" in five policy areas.

The findings for Italy inevitably cause us to ask whether there are any significant differences between the elite sport system in Italy and those in our other sample nations which may explain the apparent lack of a relationship between policy and performance. One possibility concerns the relatively high level of autonomy enjoyed by Italian NGBs which appear to operate at a greater distance from their National Agency for Sport (CONI) than NGBs in other nations. Among the sample nations, Italian NGBs received the highest overall level of public funding per organisation and the second highest level for the purposes of elite sport. It may be that a greater degree of sport-specific analysis is needed to complete our understanding of the elite sport development process in different nations.

Whereas Italy and Belgium appear at opposite ends of our performance spectrum, the UK and the Netherlands are within one place of each other on all our indices other than the overall World Sporting Index. Interestingly, there are also some notable similarities in the UK and Dutch scores in our evaluation of policy, both nations achieving a top rating in Pillar 5 (Athletic & Post-Career Support) and Pillar 8 (International Competition). A possible theory for these scores being both similar and high is that the Netherlands and the UK have only recently adopted a strategic approach to elite sport (1993 and 1997 respectively). One of the advantages of relatively late adoption is that it may be possible to benefit from the learning curve of other nations which might be described as 'early adopters' such as Australia.

---

8   As has been emphasised several times in this book, a number of significant funding and structural changes have been made in Flanders and Wallonia in recent years. However, it is too early to evaluate these changes in terms of the international performance of Belgian athletes

Certainly in the case of the UK the support for elite sport system was based on the Australian Institute for Sport model which itself had recently moved away from a centralised to a decentralised structure. Sports administrators in the UK learnt from the Australian model and implemented a regional model from the outset rather than the originally planned centralised 'flagship' approach. These findings and their explanations are inconclusive in determining whether there is a relationship between the quality of elite sport systems and nations' performance in international sport.

The remaining two nations in our sample are those with particular strength in winter sports Canada and Norway. Of the two, Canada is generally the stronger performer across our range of performance indices, but scores generally less well than Norway in terms of policy evaluation. Once again we have a finding that raises questions about the relationship between policy and performance.

As we have already indicated, Canada may be the sample nation that suffers most from the fact that our analysis focuses on national-level development and generally ignores activity at the sub-national or provincial level. While issues of geography are always likely to ensure that the provinces remain significant players in Canadian sport, it will be interesting to see whether the 2010 Vancouver Winter Olympics provide a catalyst for a more coordinated, national approach to elite sport development.

Norway took action to address concerns about national sporting performances somewhat earlier than the UK and the Netherlands (i.e. after the 1984 Sarajevo Winter Olympics). The indications are that the catalyst for progress in this nation was the establishment of a dedicated elite sport organisation (Olympiatoppen), which has managed to create a positive elite sport climate[9] with only limited resources[10]. At the same time, it is worth pointing out that, although Norway exceeds expectation on indices concerned with winter Olympic sports, its recent performance in Torino 2006[11] gives an insight into the volatility of success that smaller nations can experience. This finding gives credence (albeit anecdotal at this stage) to our assertion that in a global sporting arms race, simply maintaining performance in a climate of increased demand for success and diminishing returns on investment is a laudable achievement.

Possible drivers of an effective system

Although the above findings are inconclusive in determining whether there is a relationship between the quality of elite sport systems and nations' performance in international sport, we have looked to see whether there are any alternative methods of analysing our data which may

---

9   The Norwegian system was rated more highly by its athletes and coaches than was the system in any other nation in the study

10   Norway achieves only low scores for Pillar 1, where its overall national expenditure on sport is rated only as "low" and levels of support for national governing bodies are assessed as "little or no investment"

11   Norway won only 2 gold medals in Torino, compared with 13 in Salt Lake City 2002

prove instructive. When we focus on nations' performance in the Athens Olympics, we see that the three most successful sample nations were Italy, UK and the Netherlands. Looking at these three nations as a group, we see that the policy areas in which they achieved the highest collective rating, and thereby distinguishing themselves from the other sample nations, were Pillar 1b (funding for national governing bodies) and Pillar 7 (coaching provision and coach development). In both respects, the UK achieved a "well-developed" rating here, and the Netherlands and Italy a "good" rating. It could be argued that this finding is highlighting the importance of elite sport funding and coaching as key drivers of an effective system. Furthermore it seems that all sample nations, except from Belgium, have invested increasingly in Pillar 5 ('athletic and post career support') and Pillar 6 (training facilities).

The system for the development of elite coaches seems to be relatively immature in almost all sample nations. Besides the relatively high scores on Pillar 7 found in Italy, the UK and the Netherlands, it is still difficult for coaches to carry out the role on a full-time basis. This is an unfortunate finding as there seems to be a collective realisation that athletes need to apply themselves full time to achieve their potential. Furthermore, the influence of access to world-class coaching is widely accepted by athletes as the most important support service that they receive. This finding is confirmed in Green and Houlihan's (2005) study in which it is stated that:

> there is an acceptance of coaching as an important, if not essential, ingredient in elite success and, more importantly, an ingredient that required status and investment was slow in developing. … the supporting services of coaching, sports science and medicine were generally an afterthought (2005, p. 175).

In the nations which took part in the survey of coaches, there tends to be a general feeling of dissatisfaction with the terms and conditions that coaches enjoy in their sporting employment. There appears to be relatively low incomes, low pension and social security arrangements and poor mechanisms for the combination of coaching and other paid work. To counter these problems there seems to have been an increasing process of professionalisation of coaching careers notable in the UK and the Netherlands. The net effect of this professionalisation, the ease of worker migration and the increasing acceptance of 'foreign' coaches has created a global market for elite coaches and Performance Directors. This is yet further evidence of how the global sporting arms race is escalating.

Talent identification and development

Whether one supports these arguments or not, there is one finding that stands out clearly within our analysis. Pillar 4, Talent identification and development, is relatively under developed in most nations. No nation receives a 'policy area well developed' score on this pillar and four nations are rated as having a 'limited development' on Pillar 4. Although much more in depth analysis at the sport specific level is necessary, this finding may suggest that an effective manner by which smaller nations can gain competitive advantage is via talent identification and development. Although in population terms they were the two largest nations in our sample, Italy and the UK achieved relatively poor ratings in terms of their talent identification and development systems. What this finding may be showing is that nations with larger populations and/or a good track record of success have, historically, taken a relatively relaxed approach to talent development, believing that talent will emerge naturally. In an increasingly competitive environment, the likelihood is that an approach of this type will no longer be sustainable and that more attention will need to be paid to this important phase of the athlete development process. The performance and policy analysis of Italy supports this analysis. Although Italy continues to be one of the more successful of our sample nations, its lead has been narrowing over the last ten years. In the 1996 Atlanta Olympics, Italy finished 6th in the medal table with a market share of 4.3% of the medal points available. At Sydney, Italy fell one place in the medal table and its market share of medal points fell to 3.7%. By 2004, Italy had dropped again to 8th in the Athens medal table and its market share had fallen to 3.4%. If larger nations take a more systematic approach towards talent development, the future prospects for smaller nations are poor as they will find it even more difficult to compete in the escalating global sporting arms race.

In terms of indicating where nations might be able to derive a source of differentiation and competitive advantage in talent development we need to look historically to the former Eastern bloc and more recently to Australia. The key sports development feature in these nations is a 'system-related' scientific selection system whereby potential elite athletes are identified from outside a given sport's participant base. No nation in the sample has such an approach, yet it has

been a key feature of nations that have 'punched above their weight' in sporting performance. The potential benefits of 'system-related' selection and early detection of sporting talent highlights the importance of time as a factor in the production of elite athletes. Consistent success is not a short term 'quick fix' that can be achieved by throwing money at sport. Long-term athlete development programmes work on the rule of thumb that it takes ten years and 10,000 hours of deliberate practice to become an elite performer - and even then there is no guarantee of success. Embracing such programmes in order to improve the probability of an increased flow of elite athletes rather than simply helping athletes who have reached the top of their sport is resource-intensive and endorses the notion that there is a global sporting arms race.

Final thoughts

In terms of input-output analysis, the best predictor of output appears to be the absolute amount of funding allocated to elite sport. Relative funding measures such as funding per capita are not really relevant as output (international sporting success) is measured in absolute rather than relative terms. Australians working in elite sport have often said in simple terms that, when looking at the relationship between investment and success, 'more money in equals more medals out'. Putting these findings into context and trying to find possible explanations we can identify three key points.

1. International competition has increased and it is becoming increasingly difficult for nations to increase their market share of international sporting success.

2. Other nations have responded to seeing their success in international sport decline by increasing the amount of money they spend on elite sport, thereby fuelling an escalating global sporting arms race.

3. The input-output model proposed in this research may be too rational and economic. It is possible that elite sporting success appears to be the outcome of a multivariate process involving many variables and relationships that we are yet to discover. An alternative view is that elite sport is not a rational process and that the metaphor of an arms race is particularly apt as there is no end game other than the domination of rivals regardless of cost.

There is a paradox inherent in the discussion throughout this chapter. That is, increasing global competition is encouraging nations to adopt a more strategic elite sports policy in order to differentiate themselves from other nations with the net result being an increasingly homogenous elite sports development system which is ostensibly based around a near uniform model of elite sports development with subtle local variations. Despite attempts by governments to rationalise elite sport and to treat it like a mainstream area of government policy, the reality is that international sport is a global issue not a national issue. Consequently the rules of the game are dictated by what rival nations are doing, not on the basis of what an individual nation is doing now compared with what it did in the past. The key question facing all nations taking a strategic approach to elite sport is "to what extent do you wish to be part of this game?"

Reference List

Afonso, A., Schuknecht, L., Tanzi V. (2003). Public sector efficiency: an international comparison'. European Central Bank Working paper series, July 2003.

Anderson, D., Morris, T. (2000). Athlete lifestyle programs. In D. Lavallee, &P. Wylleman, (Eds.) *Career transitions in sport: International perspectives.* Morgantown, WV: FIT., 59-80.

Anciaux (2004). Beleidsplan 2004-2009. [Policy plan 2004-2009]. Brussels: Flemish Government.

Ball, D.W. (1972). Olympic games competition. Structural correlates of national success. *International Journal of Comparative sociology, 13* (3-4) 186-200.

Bernard, A.B., & Busse, M.R. (2000). *Who wins the Olympic Games: Economic development and medal totals.* Available at: *http://papers.ssrn.com* [online document assessed 20 October 2000].

Bloom, B.S. (1985). *Developing talent in young people.* New York: Balantine.

Broom, E.F. (1986). Funding the development of the Olympic athletes: a comparison of programs in Selected Western and socialist nations. *In Proceedings of the third International Seminar on comparative physical education and sport*, April 21-25, 1986 (pp. 21-24). Champaign: Human kinetics

Broom, E.F. (1991) Lifestyles of Aspiring High Performance Athletes: a comparison of national models. *Journal of Comparative Physical Education and Sport, 8* (2), 24-54

Buggel, E. (1986). The development of Sport in the German Democratic Republic: 1950-1985. In Proceedings of the third International Seminar on comparative physical education and sport, April 21-25, 1986, (pp. 37-53). Champaign: Human kinetics.

Chalip (1995). Policy Analysis in Sport Management, *Journal of Sport Management, 9*, 1-13.

Chelladurai, P. (2001). *Managing organisations. For sport & physical activity. A system perspective.* Scotsdale: Holcomb Hathaway publishers.

Clarke, S.R. (2002). *Home advantage in the Olympic Games.* Retrieved 27 November 2003, from *http://www.swo,/edu.au/sport/olympics/HAOlympicgames.pdf.* Swinnburn, University of Technology.

Clumpner, R.A. (1994). 21ste century success in international competition. In R. Wilcox (Ed.), Sport in the global village (pp.298-303). Morgantown, WV: FIT.

Conzelmann, A., & Nagel, S. (2003). Professional careers of the German Olympic athletes. *International Review for the Sociology of Sport, 38*, 259-280.

Copps, S. (2004). We need a lottery for amateur sport. National post. Retrieved, January 2006 from *www.Canada.com* network.

Crespo, M., Miley, D.,& Couraud, F. (2001-). An overall vision of player development. In M. Crespo, M. Reid, & D. Miley (Eds). *Tennis Player Development*, (pp.13-18). London: ITF Ltd.

De Bosscher, V., De Knop, P. (2002). The influence of sports policies on international success: An international comparative study. *In IOC (Ed.), Proceedings of the 9th World Sport for All Congress. 'Sport for All and Elite Sport: rivals or partners?* (pp.31). Ahrnem (Netherlands): International Olympic Committee.

De Bosscher, V., De Knop, P., Heyndels, B. (2003a). Comparing relative sporting success among nations: create equal opportunities in sport. *Journal for Comparative Physical Education and Sport, 3* (3) 109-120.

De Bosscher, V., De Knop, P., Heyndels, B. (2003b). Comparing tennis success among nations. *International sport studies, 1*, 49-69.

De Bosscher V., De Knop P., Van Bottenburg, M., Shibli, S. (forthcoming). Theoretical model of factors determining international sporting success. *European Sport Management Quarterly.*

De Knop, P, De Bosscher, V., & Leblicq, S., (2004). *Topsportklimaat in Vlaanderen* [elite sports climate in Flanders]. Brussel: Vrije Universiteit Brussel.

De Knop P., De Bosscher V., Van Bottenburg, M., Leblicq S. (2004). Why the Netherlands are successful and Belgium is not? A comparison of the elite sports climate and policies. *Proceedings of the 12th Congress of the European Association for Sport Management,* Ghent, 239-241.

De Smedt, E. (2001). *Atletenmanagement* [Management of athletes]. Presentation during course Vleckho business school, 31-05-01.

Digel, H. (2001). Talentsuche und talentfoerderung im internationalen vergleich [Talent detection and talent development in international comparison] *Leistungssport, 31,* 4, 72-78.

Digel, H., Burk, V. & Sloboda, H. (2003). *Hochleistungssport in Großbritannien und Nordirland.* Weilheim/Teck: Bräuer.

Digel, H., Miao, J. & Utz, A. (2003): *Hochleistungssport in China.* Weilheim/Teck: Bräuer.

Digel, H. & Kruse, A. (2004): *Hochleistungssport in Australien.* Weilheim/Teck: Bräuer.

Digel, H. & Barra, M. (2004): *Hochleistungssport in Italien.* Weilheim/Teck: Bräuer.

Digel, H., Burk, V. & Fahrrer, M. (2006): *High Performance Sport. An International Comparison.* Weilheim/Teck: Bräuer.

Duffy, P., Lyons, D., Moran, A., Warrington, G., & Macmanus, C. (2001). *Factors promoting and inhibiting the success of high performance players and athletes in Ireland.* Retrieved 20 January 2002 from: *http://www.nctc.ul.ie/press/pubs/Success%20Factors%20STUDY.doc.* National coaching & Training Centre: Ireland.

Duffy, P. (2000). Report on study visit to Australia, 18-30 September 1999. National Coaching and Training Centre: Ireland Available at: *http://www.nctc.ul.ie/press/pubs/Australia%20report.doc*

Elphinston, B. (2004). *Win to win models in Sport. The Australian Experience 1896-2004.* IOC-technical seminar, Warschau, 10-12 December 2004.

Fisher, R.J., Borms, J. (1990). *The search for sporting excellence.* Schorndorf: Verlag Karl Hofmann.

Gibbons, T., McConnel, A., Forster, T., Riewald, ST., Peterson, K. (2003). *Reflections on success: US Olympians describe the Success Factors and obstacles that most influenced their Olympic development.* USOC report phase II, 48p.

Greenleaf, C., Gould, D., & Diefen, K. (2001). Factors influencing Olympic performance with Atlanta and Nagano US Olympians. *Journal of applied sport psychology, 13,* 154-184.

Green, M., Houlihan, B. (2004). Advocacy coalitions and elite sport policy change in Canada and the United Kingdom. *International Review for the Sociology of sport, 39,* 4, 387-403.

Green, M., & Houlihan, B. (2005). Elite sport development. Policy learning and political priorities. London and New York: Routledge

Green, M., Oakley, B. (2001). Elite sport development systems and playing to win: uniformity and diversity in international approaches. *Leisure studies, 20,* 247-267.

Grimbel, B. (1976). Possibilities and problems in sports talent detection research. *Leistungssport, 6,* 159-167.

Grimes, A., Kelly, W., & Rubin, P. (1974). A socio-economic model of national Olympic performance. *Social science quarterly, 55*, 777-783.

Harre, D. (1982). *Trainingslehre.* [trainings methods]. Berlin: sportverlag

Heinemann, K. (1998). *Sports clubs in various European nations.* Series club of Cologne. Stuttgart: Hofmann Verlag.

Hoffmann, R., Ging, L.C., & Ramasamy, B. (2001). Public policy and Olympic success. Available at: *http://www.unim.nottingham.ac.uk/dbm/papers/2001-02.pdf.* [online document assessed 8 May 01]. Research Paper Series, University of Nottingham, Malaysia.

Houlihan, B. (1997). *Sport, Policy and Politics. A comparative analysis.* London and New York: Routledge.

Johnson, K.N., & Ali, A. (2002). *A tale of two seasons: participation and medal counts at the summer and winter Olympic Games.* Retrieved 15 February 2003 from *http://www.wellesley.edu/economics/wkpapers/wellwp_0010.pdf.* USA: Wellesley college, Massachusetts.

Hogan, K., & Norton, K. (2000). The price of Olympic Gold. *Journal of science and medicine in sport, 3* (2), 203-218

Kiviaho, P., & Mäkelä, P (1978). Olympic Success: a sum of non-material and material factors. *International Review of Sport sociology, 2*, 5-17.

Krüger, A. (1989). The sportification of the world: are there any differences left? *Journal of comparative physical education and sport, 2*, 5-6.

Kuper, G., & Sterken, E (2001). *Olympic participation and performance since 1896.* Departement economie, Universiteit Groningen (Nederland). Retrieved 23 Marc 2001 from *http://www.eco.rug.nl/ccso/quarterly/2001q1-4.pdf.*

Larose, K., & Haggerty, T.R. (1996). *Factors associated with national Olympic success: an exploratory study.* Non published Masters thesis, Universiteit Brunswick, Canada.

Levine, N. (1974). Why do nations win Olympic medals – some structural correlates of Olympic Games success. *Sociology and Social Research, 58,* 4, 353-360.

López de D'Amico, R. (2000) *Organisation and regulations in National Sport Bodies : a comparative study in artistic gymnastics.* Published doctoral thesis, Sydney University, USA: UMI.

National Audit Office (2005) UK Sport: Supporting elite athletes, The Stationery Office, Norwich.

Nys, K., De Knop, P., & De Bosscher (2002). *Prestatiebepalende factoren in topsport* [Factors determining international success in elite sports]. Unpublished Masters thesis, Brussels, Vrije Universiteit Brussel.

Oakley, B. and Green, M. (2001a) Still playing the game at arm's length? The selective re-investment in British sport, 1995-2000, *Managing Leisure: An International Journal Vol. 6,* No. 2, pp74-94

Oakley B., & Green, M. (2001b). The production of Olympic champions: international perspectives on elite sport development system. *European Journal for Sport Management, 8*, 83 – 105.

Papadimitriou, D., Taylor, P. (2000). Organisational Effectiveness of Hellenic National Sports Organisations: a Multiple Constituency Approach. *Sport Management Review, 3*, 23-40.

Parasuraman, A., Zeithaml, V., & Berry, L. (1985). A Conceptual Model of Service Quality and its Implications for Future Research. *Journal of Marketing, 49*, Fall, 41-50

Ragin, R.(1987). The Comparative Method. *moving beyond qualitative and quantitative strategies.* Los Angeles, CA: University of California Press.

Régnier, G., Salmela, J, Russell, S.J. (1993) Talent detection and development in sport. In: Singer, R.N., Murphy, M., Tennant, K.L. (Eds) *Handbook of research on sport psychology* (pp. 290-313). New York: Macmillan publishing company.

Riordan, J. (1989) Soviet Sport and Perestroika. *Journal of Comparative physical Education and Sport, XI, 2*; 7-18.

Riordan, J. (1991). *Sport, politics and communism.* Manchester: Manchester University Press.

Riordan, J. (1994) Communist Sports Policy: the end of an Era. In: In: R. Wilcox (1994) *Sport in the global village, Fitness Information Technology* Inc: Morgantown, WV., 89-115.

Robinson, E. (1997). Youngsters with starts in their eyes/ The Financial Times, 27 October 1997.

Rogge, J (2002) The challenges of the third Millennium, Opening speech made at the International Conference on Sports Events & Economic Impact, Copenhagen, 18th April 2002

Rowe (1994). Talentdetectie in basketball. [Talent detection in basketball]. Non published doctoral thesis, Leuven, KUL.

Sedlacek, J., Matousek, R., Holcek, R., Moravec, R. (1994) The influence of the political changes on the high performance sport organisation in Czechoslovakia. In: R. Wilcox (1994) *Sport in the global village, Fitness Information Technology* Inc: Morgantown, WV., p 341-347

Semotiuk, D. (1990) East Bloc Athletics in the Glasnost Era. Journal of Comparative Physical Education and Sport, XII, 1, 26-29

SIRC (2002). *European sporting success. A study of the development of medal winning elites in five European nations.* Sheffield: Sheffield Hallam University.

Sport Canada (2006). Canadian Interuniversity Services. Retrieved, January 2006, from http://www.pch.gc.ca/sportcanada/index_e.cfm

Shaw, S., & Pooley, J. (1976). *National* success at the Olympics: an explanation. In C. Lessard, JP Massicotte & E. Leduc (Eds), *Proceedings of the 6th international Seminar: history of Physical Education and Sport,* Trois Rivieres, Quebec, 1-27.

Stamm, H., & Lamprecht, M. (2001). *Sydney 2000, the best games ever?* World Sport and Relationships of Structural Dependency. Summary of a paper presented at the 1st World Congress of the Sociology of Sport. Seoul, Korea. Retrieved 1 March 2002 from *http://www.lssfb.ch/download/ISSA_Seoul.pdf.*

Starkes, J. (2000). The road to expertise: is practice the only determinant? *International Journal of Sport Psychology, 31*, 4, 431-451.

Thibault, L., Babiak, K. (2005). Organizational Changes in Canada's Sport System: Toward an athlete-Centred approach. *European Sport Management Quarterly, 5*, 2, 105-122

Unierzyski, P., Wielinski, D., Zhanel, J. (2003). Searching for reasons for success and failure in the careers of young tennis players – a study of two individual cases. In M. Crespo, D. Miley & M. Reid (Eds.) *Proceedings of the ITF worldwide coaches symposium,* (pp. 138). Villamoura (Portugal): ITF.

van Bottenburg, M. (2000). *Het topsportklimaat in Nederland* [The elite sports climate in the Netherlands]. 's Hertogenbosch: Diopter-Janssens en van Bottenburg bv.

van Bottenburg, M. (2003). Sport for All and Elite Sport: Do they benefit one another? In IOC (Ed.), *Proceedings van het 9e world Sport for All Congress: Sport for all and elite sport: rivals or partners*, (pp. 25). Ahrnem (Netherlands): IOC.

van Bottenburg, M., Rijnen, B., and van Sterkenberg, J. (2005) *Sports participation in the European Union, trends and differences.* WJH Mulier Institute, Arko Sports Media (Netherlands).

Wells, H.J.C. (1991). Developing sporting excellence in Hong Kong. *Journal of Comparative Physical Education and Sport, 1*, 28-34.

Wylleman, P., De Knop, P., & Sillen, D. (1998). *Former Olympic athletes' perceptions of retirement from high-level sport.* Presentation during the 28e Congress of the International Association of Applied Psychology. San Francisco, US, IAAP-APA, 9-14.08.1998.

Wylleman, P., & Lavallee, D. (2003). A developmental perspective on transitions faced by athletes. In M. Weiss (Ed.), *Developmental sport and exercise psychology: A lifespan perspective.* Morgantown, WV: FIT.

APPENDIX 1: RESPONSES BY NATION AND BY SPORT FOR ATHLETES, COACHES AND PERFORMANCE DIRECTORS

ATHLETES	NATION					
SPORT	UK	NETHERLANDS	WALLONIA	FLANDERS	NORWAY	TOTALS
ADAPTED SPORTS	0	0	6	0	6	
ARCHERY	8	1	3	0	0	12
ATHLETICS	31	15	4	15	7	72
ATHLETICS (DISABILITY)	15	0	0	0	0	15
BADMINTON	0	7	6	2	1	16
BASEBALL	0	11	0	0	0	11
BASKETBALL	0	4	0	28	0	32
BEACH VOLLEYBALL	0	0	0	0	3	3
BOBSLEIGH	1	7	0	0	0	8
BRIDGE	0	3	0	0	0	3
BOCCIA	2	0	0	0	0	2
BOWLING	0	3	0	0	0	3
BOXING	0	0	1	0	2	3
CANOEING	17	9	0	4	0	30
CHESS	0	2	0	0	0	2
CLAY PIGEON SHOOTING	0	1	0	0	0	1
CLIMBING	0	3	2	0	0	5
CRICKET	0	5	0	0	0	5
CURLING	0	2	0	0	0	2
CYCLING (Track / Road / MB) (TOURING)	17	19	1	0	0	37
CYCLING	0	0	2	9	3	14
DANCE	0	8	0	0	0	8
DARTS	0	1	0	0	0	1
DIVING	4	0	0	0	0	4
DRAUGHTS	0	4	0	0	0	4
DUATHLON	0	1	0	0	0	1
EQUESTRIAN	11	4	1	4	4	24
FENCING	0	2	0	2	2	6
FOOTBALL	0	6	0	0	0	6
FOOTBALL (DISABILITY)	0	2	0	0	0	2
GOLF	0	9	0	0	0	9
GYMNASTICS	13	8	1	5	0	27

HANDBALL	0	11	0	10	0	21
HANDGLIDING	0	1	0	0	0	1
HOCKEY	0	17	0	0	0	17
ICE HOCKEY	0	11	0	0	0	11
ICE SKATING	0	0	0	0	0	0
ICE SKATING (SPEED)	1	0	8	2	0	11
JUDO	10	0	1	11	0	22
KAYAKING	0	1	7	0	6	14
KICKBOXING	0	0	0	0	2	2
LIFE-SAVING	0	0	1	2	0	3
MARTIAL ARTS	0	23	0	0	0	23
MODERN PENTATHLON	6	0	0	0	0	6
MODEL AIRPLANES	0	7	0	0	0	7
MOTORSPORT	0	8	0	0	1	9
ORIENTEERING	2	0	0	0	1	3
PARACHUTING	0	4	0	0	0	4
POWERLIFTING	0	6	1	0	0	7
POWERLIFTING (DISABILITY)	4	0	0	0	0	4
ROLLER HOCKEY	0	2	0	0	0	2
ROWING	31	25	0	2	10	68
RUGBY	0	20	2	0	0	22
SAIL FLYING	0	2	0	0	0	2
SAILING	20	0	10	0	1	31
SHOOTING	8	8	1	0	6	23
SHOOTING (DISABILITY)	5	0	0	0	0	5
SKATING	0	11	0	0	0	11
SKIING /SNOWBOARDING	0	4	1	0	0	5
SNOOKER/POOL	0	13	0	0	2	15
SQUASH	0	4	0	1	0	5
SWIMMING	17	26	0	4	2	49
SWIMMING (DISABILITY)	14	0	0	0	0	14
TABLE TENNIS	0	7	0	0	1	8
TABLE TENNIS (DISABILITY)	6	1	0	0	0	7
TAE KWON DO	2	0	2	0	1	5
TENNIS	0	1	0	1	0	2
TENNIS (DISABILITY)	5	1	0	0	0	6
TRAMPOLINING	3	4	1	0	0	8

APPENDICES

TRIATHLON	5	7	1	6	0	19
TUG OF WAR	0	3	0	0	0	3
WATER SKIING	3	0	2	5	0	10
WATERPOLO	0	16	0	0	0	16
WATERSPORT	0	19	0	0	0	19
WHEELCHAIR BASKETBALL	5	0	0	0	8	13
WHEELCHAIR DANCE	3	0	0	0	0	3
WHEELCHAIR RUGBY	10	0	0	0	0	10
WINDSURFING	0	0	2	5	0	7
WRESTLING	0	0	2	0	0	2
VOLLEYBALL	0	9	0	15	0	24
VOLLEYBALL (DISABILITY)	0	4	0	0	0	4
2 SPORTS (UNSPECIFIED)	0	1	0	0	0	1
TOTALS	**279**	**422**	**63**	**139**	**55**	**958**

COACHES SPORT	NATION UK	NETHERLANDS	WALLONIA	FLANDERS	ITALY	TOTAL
ARCHERY	0	0	1	0	0	1
ATHLETICS	3	4	6	16	2	31
ATHLETICS (DISABILITY)	1	0	0	0	0	1
BADMINTON	0	1	1	3	0	5
BASEBALL	1	0	0	0	3	4
BASKETBALL	0	2	0	9	0	11
BOCCIA	1	0	0	0	0	1
BOWLING	0	2	0	0	0	2
BRIDGE	0	1	0	0	0	1
CANOEING	1	1	0	1	2	5
CHESS	0	1	0	0	0	1
CLIMBING	0	0	1	0	0	1
CRICKET	0	1	0	0	0	1
CYCLING (DISABILITY)	1	0	0	0	0	1
CYCLING (TOURING)	1	0	0	3	3	7
DRAUGHTS	0	1	0	0	0	1
EQUESTRIAN / RIDING	1	1	0	5	0	7
FENCING	0	2	0	5	1	8
FOOTBALL (FIELD)	0	2	0	0	0	2
GYMNASTICS	0	2	2	17	1	22
HANDBALL	0	1	0	6	0	7
HOCKEY	1	2	0	0	2	5
ICE HOCKEY	0	1	0	0	3	4
ICE SKATING	0	0	0	1	2	3
JUDO	0	0	0	7	0	7
KAYAKING	0	0	0	1	0	1
LIFE-SAVING	0	0	1	0	0	1
MARTIAL ARTS	0	5	0	0	0	5
MODERN PENTATHLON	0	1	0	0	0	1
ORIENTEERING	1	0	0	0	1	2
POWERLIFTING	0	0	1	0	0	1
ROLLER HOCKEY	0	0	0	0	1	1
ROWING	0	2	0	4	1	7
RUGBY	0	0	0	0	2	2
SAILING	1	0	2	0	2	5
SHOOTING	0	3	0	2	0	5
SKATING (ANY)	0	3	0	0	0	3

SKIING /SNOWBOARDING	0	3	0	3	4	10
SNOOKER/POOL	0	2	0	0	0	2
SWIMMING	2	5	0	1	0	8
TABLE TENNIS	0	1	0	5	0	6
TAEKWONDO	0	0	0	2	0	2
TENNIS	0	1	2	11	1	15
TRIATHLON	2	2	0	0	0	4
VOLLEYBALL	0	2	0	10	1	13
WATER SKIING	2	0	0	0	0	2
WATERPOLO	0	2	0	0	0	2
WATERSPORT	0	5	0	0	0	5
WHEELCHAIR BASKETBALL	2	0	0	0	0	2
WINDSURFING	0	0	0	2	0	2
MISSING / NOT STATED	2	0	0	1	0	3
ADAPTED / DISABILITY	0	0	0	3	0	3
PHYSIO (i.e. NOT COACH)	0	0	0	1	0	1
TOTALS	**23**	**62**	**17**	**119**	**32**	**253**

PERFORMANCE DIRECTORS					
SPORT	NETHERLANDS	WALLONIA	FLANDERS	CANADA	TOTAL
ARCHERY			1		1
ATHLETICS		2	1		3
BADMINTON			1		1
BASKETBALL			2		2
CANOING		1	1		2
CYCLING (TOURING)			1		1
EQUESTRIAN / RIDING			1		1
FENCING		1	1		2
GYMNASTICS			1		1
HANDBALL			1		1
JUDO			1		1
LIFE-SAVING			1		1
ROWING			1		1
SHOOTING			1		1
SKATING			1		1
SQUASH			1		1
SWIMMING			1		1
TABLE TENNIS			1		1
TAE KWON DO			1		1
TENNIS		1	1		2
TRIATHLON			1		1
VOLLEYBALL			1		1
WATER SKIING			1		1
YACHTING		1	1		2
ADAPTED / DISABILITY			1		1
MISSING / NOT STATED	28			11	39
TOTALS	28	6	26	11	71

APPENDIX 2: THE SCORING SYSTEM METHODOLOGY

This appendix provides further detail on the methodology employed to develop the scoring system in the SPLISS study and was devised as part of a PhD. study by Veerle de Bosscher from the Vrije Universiteit Brussel (VUB- University Brussels). This scoring system will be illustrated in the form of a worked example using Pillar 2 i.e. sport policy structures and organisation. This pillar, probably one of the most difficult ones in terms of defining the critical success factors, was selected because it involves data collected from all areas of the study's methods. For more detailed information regarding the other pillars, please contact Veerle De Bosscher: *vdebossc@vub.ac.be*

In the following section the general methodology of the scoring system is explained using sequential steps. The scoring system aims to express the general assessment of each pillar for each nation by consolidating different criteria into one final percentage score. De Pelsmacker and Van Kenhove (1999) suggest these steps as a typical methodology for measuring competitiveness in market research. The final score derived from such a system enables the analysis and interpretation of results to go beyond the descriptive level of comparison.

Step 1: Determine the Critical Success Factors
The success criteria as identified in chapter three of this book that were subsequently operationalised into measurement questions are our critical success factors (CSF). The data required to measure these CSFs were collected through two measurement instruments: (1) the overall sport policy questionnaire and (2) the elite sport climate survey questionnaires filled in by athletes, coaches and Performance Directors. A total of 105 indicators have been included in the scoring system. It was decided to separate the scores for 'facts', which give an objective measurement, from 'assessments', which were a subjective measurement of the CSF. The former were derived from both the overall sport policy questionnaire and the elite sport climate survey, whereas the latter were derived from the elite sport climate survey only. The main reason for this distinction was that not all 'facts' were assessed and the assessment did not always reflect the whole pillar.

Step 2: Determine the scores for each CSF
To develop a score, each CSF was ranked on a five point scale. Depending on the source (elite sport climate survey or overall sport policy questionnaire) and kind of question (dichotomous or assessment), this scale differed. Generally there were three kinds of ratings.

1. In the overall policy questionnaire qualitative information on the elite sport systems for each pillar had to be translated into a score for a five point scale. A lack of existing information did not permit these standards to be developed in advance and had to be developed after the data collection phase. For each CSF the standards and ratings were discussed within the consortium group.

    Generally, the existence of specific aspects of the elite sport system was assessed in terms of 'availability of the criterion in a stronger or weaker form'. This is presented in the following table as a continuum.

	Points
Poor or no level of development	1
…	2
Moderate level of development	3
…	4
Strong level of development	5

The evaluation of pillar 1 (financial support) differed in this respect. Here nations were scored in relation to survey averages.

An example of the attribution of scores for open ended questions from the overall sport policy questionnaire is given below.

Coordination of expenditures and activities at national level (horizontal direction): expenditures on elite sport at the national level are centrally recorded and coordinated, so that no overlap takes place

score

	score	
High level of coordination: there is mainly one organisation at national level which makes decisions about the majority of expenditure and activities in elite sport; eventually the Olympic Committee is merged with the national sport administration	5	Italy: CONI coordinates all money flows at national level; Norway - Olympiatoppen: idem (except for the NGB's in football and skiing, which have enough money on their own). Furthermore, the current NOC, was formed in 1996 following an amalgamation of the Norwegian Olympic Committee and Confederation of Sports; the Netherlands: NOC*NSF is a fusion of the sport administration and Olympic Committee; NOC*NSF coordinates expenditures from SNS (lottery funding) and VWS (Ministry); responsibilities are delineated transparently to ensure clarity of purpose and to avoid duplication; UK Sport is the most influential agency in the UK regarding expenditure on elite sport; The British Olympic Association focuses primarily on the selection and preparation of the Great Britain Olympic team, and the British Paralympic Association operates in similar terms in relation to the Paralympic team.
Reasonable level of national coordination: there is more than one organisation at national level spending money (independently) on elite sport, but there is a coordination between these agencies so that expenditures and activities are delineated transparently to avoid duplication	3	Flanders: BOIC, Bloso and Minister all spend money on elite sport; these have been coordinated by a steering group since 2003; in Canada elite sport is mainly the responsibility of Sport Canada and also the COC (Olympic Committee), have meetings to delineate responsibilities and expenditures.
Low level of national coordination: there is more than one organisation at national level spending money on elite sport; this is not recorded and not centralised; it is not known approximately how much money NGBs and athletes in the nation receive at national level	1	In Wallonia there is no coordinating agency for the activities of Adeps and BOIC; Adeps has no elite sport department; expenditures on elite sport from different organisations are not nationally coordinated or recorded.

Figure A1: An illustration of the points attributed to open ended (qualitative) questions from the overall sport policy questionnaire:

2. In the elite sports climate survey quantitative data were available based on two kinds of questions: dichotomous questions (yes/no) and ratings on a five point Likert scale (ordinal)[12]. For the dichotomous questions absolute standards were used and for the Likert scale questions 'net ratings' (i.e. positive answers minus negative answers) were used. An example of how the system was used in practice is shown below.

Dichotomous questions (yes/no)		Ratings	
% yes	Points	% (pos. – neg.)	evaluation
0-20%	1 (—)	<-20%	1 (—)
21-40%	2 (-)	(-1)–(-20)%	2 (-)
41-60%	3 (0)	0-20%	3 (0)
61-80%	4 (+)	21-50%	4 (+)
81-100%	5 (++)	>50%	5 (++)

The figure below provides an example of a score calculation for a dichotomous question for pillar 2.

	N	%	score
Flanders	138	10,87	1
The Netherlands	417	35,01	2
Norway	55	21,82	2
Canada	120	76,67	4

Figure A2: An illustration of a dichotomous question for pillar 2: Does your NGB have an Athletes Commission? (according to athletes and taken from the athletes' elite sport climate survey)

An example of net rating calculation for pillar 2 is:

	N	++ (A)	+ (B)	0	- (C)	— (D)	Satisfaction (A+B) - (C+D)	score
Flanders	126	9,5%	34,1%	30,2%	17,5%	8,7%	8,7%	3
The Netherlands	414	18,4%	39,1%	27,5%	9,2%	5,8%	3,4%	4
Norway	54	25,9%	24,1%	38,9%	7,4%	3,7%	3,7%	4
Wallonia	58	5,2%	27,6%	25,9%	25,9%	15,5%	10,3%	3

Figure A3: An illustration of a net rating question for pillar 2: How do you assess the supply of information from your governing body? (according to athletes)

Criteria were weighted to reflect our view of their relative importance. These weightings were discussed and agreed for each pillar by the SPLISS consortium group. This methodology is not new and has been considered suitable for enhancing internal validity in market research (De Pelsmacker & Van Kenhove, 1999).

---

12   An example of a dichotomous question: "Can you make use of the following provisions? …"
    An example of a rating: "how do you rate the extra attention you have received as an emerging young talent from your governing body" (good – satisfactory – reasonable – unsatisfactory – poor)

Step 4: calculate the total score for each pillar: traffic lights

In the next step, an overall percentage score was calculated taking into account the number of 'non available' (n/a) answers, as not all nations have a score on the same number of criteria. When two thirds of the answers were not available for any nation, a score for that pillar was not calculated. When only two nations responded to a criterion, the criterion was deleted. A final percentage score was then calculated, which ranged from 20% - 100%. Scores lower than 20% are not possible as each nation received at least 1 point for each CSF. This 80% range was divided over a five point scale, with a 16% range between each category. Using these scales each nation was allocated a colour coded score or 'traffic light', varying from green for a policy area very well developed and red for little or no development as shown in the Figure below.

Total score (%)	evaluation	
84.01-100%	Policy area very well developed	
68.01-84.00%	Good level of development	
52.01-68.00%	Moderate level of development	
36.01-52.00%	Limited development	
20.00-36.00%	Little or no development	

Figure A4: Traffic light score calculation

Finally, the figure below gives an illustration of the total score development for each nation against Pillar 2.

A. General score of pillar 2 on "facts"

W	Critical Success Factors (CSF)	CAN	FI	IT	NI	NOR	UK	WAL
	Organisation of sports and policies							
1	There is a ministry and/or minister of sport	2	5	2	4	2	4	5
2	There is an organisation at national level with specific responsibilities for elite sport (as a core task)	3	3	3	3	5	5	3
2	Coordination of expenditures and activities at national level (horizontal)	3	3	5	5	5	5	1
2	Coordination of expenditures and activities at regional level (vertical)	1	5	5	5	5	3	5
	Simplicity of administration							
1	Public sector efficiency (European Central Bank, 2003)	3	*scores on a 1-5 scale questions deriving from the overall policy questionnaire*		2	4	4	2
	Targeting of key sports and elite sports							
1	The number of recognised and funded NGBs for sport	5	4	3	3	5	1	4
1	The number of recognised and funded NGBs for elite sport purposes	3	5	3	2	5	4	4
	Effective communication: an unbroken line up through all levels of elite sports policies							
2	Provision of information to national governing bodies to develop their management capability	4			5	4	5	1
1	Athletes commission in national governing bodies	4	*scores on a 1-5 scale questions deriving from the elite sport climate survey: dichotomous questions*		2	2	na	na
1	Information received from governing bodies acc. to athletes	4			4	3	na: not available	
1	Information received from governing bodies acc. to coaches	na			4	na	na	na
	TOTAL points	43	50	42	57	59	54	35
	MAX number of times NA	70 1	75 0	65 2	75 0	70 1	65 2	60 3
	Total score for pillar 2	61,43	66,67	64,62	76,00	84,29	83,08	58,33

W Weights for each CSF

Sum of (the points for each nation x weight)

Maximum score that each nation can have, taking into account the number of 'non available' anwers (=weight for each CSF x 5)

Percentage scores = total points/MAX

na: data not available; W: weight
blue text: results from elite sports climate survey

B. General score of pillar 2 on "assessment"

W		CAN	FL	IT	NI	NOR	UK	WAL
1	Supply of information from NGB - athletes' satisfaction				4	4	na	2
1	Supply of information from NGB - coaches' satisfaction	*scores on a 1-5 scale questions deriving from the elite sport climate survey: based on net ratings*			5	na	na	na
1	Involvement in policy from NGB - athletes' satisfaction				2	3	1	na
1	Involvement in policy from NGB - coaches' satisfaction				5	na	na	na
	TOTAL points for assessment	3	8	5	16	7	1	2
	Max	5	20	10	20	10	5	5
	number of times NA	3	0	2	0	2	3	3
	Total score for assessment of pillar 2	na	40,00	50,00	80,00	70,00	na	na

CAN	Canada
FL	Flanders
IT	Italy
NL	The Netherlands
NOR	Norway
UK	United Kingdom
WALL	Wallony

Figure A5: An illustration of pillar two regarding the methodology used for development of a scoring system.

The evaluation and assessment of each pillar were deliberately kept separate and were reported separately as shown in Figure A6 below.

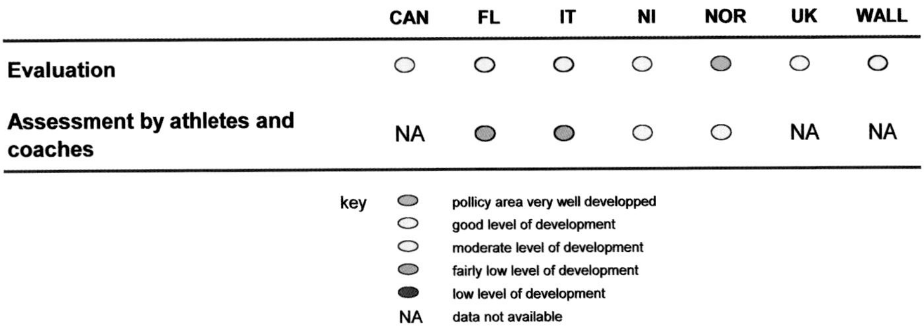

	CAN	FL	IT	NI	NOR	UK	WALL
Evaluation	○	○	○	○	◉	○	○
Assessment by athletes and coaches	NA	◔	◑	○	○	NA	NA

key
- ○ pollicy area very well developped
- ○ good level of development
- ○ moderate level of development
- ◔ fairly low level of development
- ● low level of development
- NA data not available

Figure A6

For Pillar 2 this worked example of the scoring system methodology has shown how 12 evaluation criteria and four assessment criteria were each reduced to one colour coded score, or traffic light. A similar approach was taken for the other eight pillars which in turn provided the data necessary to compile Tables 6.3 and 6.4 in the main body of the text.

APPENDIX 3: BACKGROUND INFORMATION ON SPORTS POLICY AND STRUCTURES IN THE PARTICIPATING NATIONS

Belgium

Belgium comprises three communities: Flemish, French and German-speaking. The Flemish part is known as Flanders (around 6 million inhabitants), while the French and German-speaking parts together make up Wallonia (around 4 million inhabitants). In both Flanders and Wallonia, sport is a responsibility of the department of culture and is coordinated by the sports administrative bodies, respectively Bloso and Adeps. Both communities have their own regulations, their own laws (which are called decrees at a community level), and their own system for recognition of sports and governing bodies and municipalities. For these reasons, Flanders and Wallonia have been dealt with separately within this study.

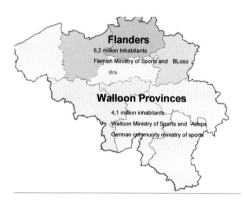

While most sports governing bodies have separate branches for Flanders and Wallonia, some continue to operate at a pan-Belgian level e.g. Royal Belgian Soccer Federation (KBVB) and the Belgian Hockey Federation. Sports such as these are neither governed, regulated nor funded at a Flanders (or Wallonia) level. A national (Belgian) governing body is necessary for representation on international federations and for the participation of Belgian teams and athletes in international championships.

National Olympic Committee: BOIC

The BOIC is the representative Olympic Committee for the whole of Belgium. In international events, athletes represent Belgium – not Wallonia or Flanders separately. This situation has certain policy implications. The BOIC helps to meet any shortfall in the support provided by Bloso and Adeps for elite athletes and governing bodies. For example, since 2003, BOIC has provided funds (€20,000 per athlete) enabling governing bodies to provide sport technical support to elite athletes at high school/university level.

ABCD

Twice a year and Adeps (Wallonia), Bloso (Flanders), BOIC and the German community have a national meeting, which is called ABCD and where topics of national importance are discussed.

National lottery funding for sporting, cultural and welfare purposes in Belgium amounted to €65.9 million in 2003. BOIC receives €1.86 million per annum from the Lottery. In future, ABCD will receive €3.25 million per annum for 10 years to support the identification of young talent, with the aim of enhancing medal chances in 2012.

Private sector

Although the FESI (Federation of European Sports Industry) has its office in Brussels, there is no sports industry federation in Belgium. There are a number of local initiatives to promote sport and elite sports, one example being Randstad Sport. This is an employment agency, operating primarily in Flanders. This organisation tries to integrate and prepare elite athletes and ex-elite athletes for employment, by providing education (Randstad Sport Academy), career planning and job creation. However, its role is limited and is far more developed in the Netherlands.

A. Flanders

Historical background

After 30 years in which there was little policy change in elite sport in Flanders, there have recently been a number of developments:

- Total public expenditure on sport has increased by 41% and expenditure on elite sport has more than doubled over the last five years
- Significant efforts are being made to improve the efficiency and effectiveness of sports governing bodies. More transparent criteria have been introduced for the recognition, funding and technical support of governing bodies, with emphasis being put on the development of quality-oriented policies and services.
- A range of measures have been introduced to support for athletes, including an employment contract (1995); elite sport and study schools (1998); and support (sport technical and study) in high school/universities (2003)
- An elite sport department has been established at Bloso and a steering committee for elite sport set up.

The latter development is regarded as one of the most important changes in addressing the inefficiencies inherent in the previous system.

Current sport structures

National government

The national administrative body for sport (including elite sport) in the Flemish Community is Bloso. Although autonomous in policy terms, 86% of Bloso's budget comprises government funding.

As far as elite sport is concerned, the main tasks of Bloso and the department of elite sport are (1) recognition and funding of (elite) sports governing bodies and support regarding technical-, medical-, paramedical and psychological services; (2) financial support of athletes through employment contracts; (3) coordination and financial support of elite sport schools, for the combination of top sport and study both at secondary and high school level; (4) development of the elite sport infrastructure and (5) development of (elite sport) coaches through the Flemish trainers school (VTS: an autonomous department of Bloso).

In addition to Bloso, the Ministry of Culture, Media and Sport of the Flemish Community has its own Department of Youth and Sport, founded in 2000. Although this Department has no major role to play in elite sport policy overall, it does deal with requests for funding in connection with international events in Flanders. Furthermore it provides financial support to a professional cycling team 'Flanders', a female cycling team 'Flanders' and (until 2004) an athletics team.

In 2003, a steering committee was set up to address a perceived lack of coordination between Bloso, the Department of Youth & Sport, BOIC and VSF. Up to 2005, the Committee was chaired mainly by Bloso but in October 2004 the Minister of Sport decided that a separate manager should be identified to lead it.

National governing bodies
The Flemish Sports Federation (VSF) is an umbrella organization of 88 governing bodies (of which 68 are publicly funded - 26 for elite sport purposes). The VSF is the main representative organization for governing bodies seeking to influence national governmental policy.

Local government (municipalities and provinces)
Municipalities and provinces play little part in supporting elite sport, their role being confined primarily to the development of facilities and the general sports infrastructure. However, some cities, such as Antwerp, are keen to present an image as an elite sports centre and have recently provided separate funds for elite sport.

Lotteries
In 2003, the Flemish Community received €38.9 million from the National Lottery. 36% of these funds are allocated to sport (Bloso: €12.4 million, BOIC: €1.86 million Euros). This means that 14.3% of the total sport budget derives from lotteries.

B. Wallonia

Current sport structures

The structure of sport in Wallonia is comparable to that in Flanders. Given the small number of inhabitants in the German-speaking community, sport is organised jointly between the French and German-speaking communities, with relevant clubs and governing bodies being mostly affiliated to Adeps.

National government

Adeps is the administrative body for sport in Wallonia, the equivalent of Bloso in Flanders. The four priorities for sport in the French speaking community are:

* development of athletes and coaches
* promoting sports
* anti-doping campaigns
* elite sports policies

The department concerned with elite sports policy is responsible for:

* permanant centres for elite sport training
* funding of governing bodies and individual athletes
* representing the German-speaking community in ABCD
* promoting scientific research and agreements with universities
* international relations
* coordinating an educational programme for sports managers

National governing bodies

Adeps recognises 64 governing bodies, which are classified in one of three funding categories related to the profile of their sport. 36 governing bodies in categories 1 and 2 receive funding for elite sport purposes.

As in Flanders, there is an umbrella organisation for Walloon governing bodies: AISF (Association Interfédérale du Sport Francophone). 58 governing bodies are affiliated to this organisation. AISF provides information, advice and assistance to its member organisations and is responsible for communication with the government.

In the German community, a "Sportrat" was established in 2002, comprising representatives from governing bodies, local sports councils and sports clubs.

Local government (municipalities and provinces)

The role of municipalities and provinces is mainly concerned with recreational sport, leisure activities and the organisation of events. There are a number of training centres where access by elite athletes is carefully managed alongside school and community use. Provinces have their own 'house of sport'.

Lotteries

In 2003, the French and German-speaking communities received € 27 million from the National Lottery.

Canada

Current Sport structures

Elite sport in Canada is structured in many respects in two separate continuums that occasionally overlap. The first is the professional sport system that includes the National Hockey League, Canadian Football League, National Basketball Association, Major League Baseball and the National Lacrosse Association. There are other smaller professional leagues as well in a variety of sports. In addition there are minor leagues in baseball and hockey predominantly.

The second pillar is amateur sport which is overseen by Sport Canada which is part of the Federal (national) government.

National government
Sport Canada is a branch of the International and Intergovernmental Affairs Sector within the *federal Department of Canadian Heritage.* Sport Canada has three divisions: Sport Programs, Sport Policy, and Major Games and Hosting. High Performance and Sport Organisations are two sections within the division of Sport Programs. Sport Canada supports the achievement of high performance and the development of the Canadian sport system to strengthen the unique contribution that sport makes to Canadian identity, culture and society. Next to this, Sport Canada provides funding for national governing bodies and many multi sport organizations (MSO).

Furthermore we should note that next to the federal funding from the Department of Heritage, funding for sport for all also comes from the Ministry of Health, which funds 'Fitness Canada'. Physical Activity, smoking, sexuality, food & nutrition, family violence, alcohol & drug abuse are, among others, responsibilities of the Ministry of Health. Physical activity focuses on getting people active (walking up stairs, getting children to play outside)

National Olympic Committee
The other significant players in elite sports in Canada are the Canadian Olympic Committee (COC) and the Canadian Paralympics Committee. They also provide financial support, services and leadership to the Canadian amateur high performance sport community and focuses on those sports within the Olympic programs.

The COC and various other partners have supported eight Sport Centres spread across the nation that provide administrative and support services for athletes living in that area. Athletes get world-class facilities and support from leading experts regarding coaching, sports medicine, strength and conditioning training, nutrition, sport psychology, exercise physiology and a range of lifestyle support services.

The COC and Sport Canada often work in parallel in trying to promote the sport system.

Lotteries
The federal government became involved in lotteries to help finance the 1976 Olympic Games in Montréal and launched the Olympic Lottery in November 1973. In 1985 an agreement between the federal government and the provinces left the field to the provinces.

National and provincial governing bodies

There are 57 national governing bodies and 25 Multi-sport Service Organisations (15 Multi Sport Agencies and 10 Service Agencies) in Canada. The governing bodies are responsible for the development of their sport and in most cases have provincial offices that receive funding directly from their provincial government. The MSO's provide a variety of services including advocacy, research, hosting of games and coordinating national teams for various events.

Most governing bodies receive a majority of their funding from the Federal Government (Sport Canada) and occasionally the COC. It is being argued that corporate Canada and other revenue streams need to be developed. The Provincial Sport Associations (PSO's) and local clubs receive money from their provincial government and lotteries. Furthermore, all have their own separate agreements with sponsors.

Local government

The role of local government in sports is important in Canada, especially at the provincial level. Provinces all have their own sports budgets and receive funds from lotteries. The Provinces and Federal government sign many bilateral agreements to develop sport (e.g. concerning lottery funding). While it is difficult to form an overall view of the role that each province plays, generally speaking the Provinces focus sport for all. However, in Quebec, national level athletes receive an additional € 3,752 per year on top of the money they receive from the federal government.

Commercial sector

An Ekos (1997) survey indicated that 44% of "carded" athletes (those athletes who receive financial support from Sport Canada) earned an average income of €4,063 per annum from sport-related sources such as a professional athlete's salary, endorsements or sponsorships, appearance fees, prize money or an athletic scholarship.

General remarks

Canada is the only nation to have hosted an Olympic Games (Montreal in 1976 and Calgary 1988) and not won a gold medal at those games.

There is little relationship between professional and amateur sport other than in instances where professional athletes (such as hockey players from the NHL) compete in Olympic Games. Funding from Sport Canada is provided through the various programs noted above. It is either provided directly to the national governing body or to the athlete in ways of carding (funding provided annually, dependent on performance achieved) and specific grants to assist with training.

After a poor performance in Athens, the Canadian Olympic Committee announced that its target is for Canada to top the medal table at the 2010 Winter Olympics in Vancouver/ Whistler. Investment in elite sport has increased accordingly.

Italy

Historical background
Prior to 1999, organisational responsibilities within Italian sport were relatively stable, with the NOC (CONI) taking a strong lead and other roles being clearly delineated. Since 1999, a number of important changes have taken place: an enhanced role for local authorities in providing the basic conditions for people to take part in sport, and a substantial growth of their competence in terms of sport for all. At the same time, a dramatic reduction in Lottery revenue has affected the support that can be provided to clubs and federations.

Other important policy changes have included athletes' and coaches' empowerment and the development of a strong anti-doping policy. Finally, at the beginning of 2004, new legislation (the so-called reform Pescante) modified the structure and remit of the NOC as well as its election procedures. The NOC, that for decades had had a broad responsibility for sport in Italy, is now more focused on elite sport. Although not an explicit policy aim, this approach appears to be widening the gap between grass-roots and top-level sport. Last but not least, there has been an increase in state intervention in sport since 1999 - especially in 2005 (see below).

Current sport structures

National Government, National Olympic Committee and lotteries
Top-level sport in Italy is primarily the responsibility of CONI, which administers the Olympic Preparation Programme through specific funding allocated to the Olympic Club and to other sub-programs. CONI owns and manages a range of National Training Centres and other scientific facilities and services. Since 1948, CONI has held exclusive gambling rights over the competitions and events for which it is responsible, and gambling/Lottery revenues have accounted for an estimated 90% of its income. Up to 2004, Government support for CONI was occasional and variable (between €60 and 125 millions per year). However, the recent decline in Lottery revenue has caused the National Government to regularise this arrangement such that CONI now receives a fixed sum of around €450 millions per year for the duration of the Olympic cycle irrespective of the revenues flowing from the lotteries.

National governing bodies
The delivery of support programmes to elite athletes is primarily the responsibility of individual national governing bodies of sport, which bid to CONI for resources. Some governing bodies also provide grants to their elite athletes to cover living expenses, while others reward success by making graded payments depending on performance achieved.

Local government
Local authorities are seldom involved in high performance sport and talent development initiatives. However, they play an important role in financing grass-roots sport, investing significantly more than the national government in this respect. Their financial have decreased since 1994.

Commercial sector
Businesses commonly enter into contractual arrangements with governing bodies and elite clubs, particularly around the Olympic Games and World or European Championship, which provide them with substantial media exposure. However there is no overall and specific policy initiative on this side. There is also no specific intervention by other commercial sport organizations as far as elite sport (outside professional clubs.).

The Netherlands
Current sport structures

The development of elite sport and elite sports policy in the Netherlands is primarily the responsibility of the national governing bodies of sport and the Netherlands' Olympic Committee* Netherlands' Sports Federation (NOC*NSF).

NOC*NSF operates both as the National Olympic Committee and as the National Sport Federation in the Netherlands. Its objective is to advance the interests of Dutch organised sport (sports for all and elite sport). The specific goal for elite sport is for the Netherlands to be one of the ten best performing nations in the world. In this regard,

therefore, NOC*NSF supports the development of "world class performance" programmes, better working conditions for athletes in the elite level squad, sports "master coach" training courses, and a "Top sport Expertise Centrum (TEC)". It also provides financial reimbursements to elite athletes and administers a fund for accommodation and training equipment. In addition, NOC*NSF provides information on doping and sexual harassment to elite athletes and distributes money from the lotteries to the different governing bodies.

NOC*NSF, as an umbrella organisation, is funded by the government and the lotteries. Funds for governing bodies are channelled through the ministry and the lotteries, but funding decisions are coordinated by NOC*NSF. For additional income, NOC*NSF and the governing bodies look to sponsors, television broadcast rights and membership fees.

National government
Through the Ministry of Health, Welfare and Sport (VWS), the national government supports elite athletes, the governing bodies and NOC*NSF to create the conditions necessary for a competitive elite sports climate. This support consists of 1) grants for elite athletes with an annual income below minimum wage; 2) funding for governing bodies with respect to national training/coaching at an elite level and to their national talent recognition and development policies; 3) support for the hosting of international elite sports events and constructing elite sports facilities; 4) funding for specific elite sports projects undertaken by NOC*NSF, for example financial assistance to the Regional Olympic Support centres.

In addition, the Ministry addresses problems related to elite sports, such as hooliganism, injuries, and drug use. The governing bodies and the sports industry are primarily responsible for addressing these problems in the Netherlands, but the national government offers support and takes the initiative if and when it is considered to be in the public interest for it to do so.

Besides the funding possibilities offered by VWS, it is sometimes possible for governing bodies and NOC*NSF to apply to other ministries for financial support. This involves, for example, sports-related areas such as the environment and education.

Lotteries
As in many other European nations, elite sport in the Netherlands is also funded by revenues generated by the national lottery (SNS). These revenues are distributed by NOC*NSF. Governing bodies can apply to NOC*NSF for lottery funding if they are affiliated to it as normal members. Some of these revenues are paid directly to the governing bodies other awards are made to umbrella sports organisations for the purpose of supporting the governing bodies.
Local government

Since the Second World War, local authorities have played a crucial role in creating conditions for sport participation, mainly through the development of sports facilities. Although support for elite sport is limited at a local level. in the 1990s several big cities sought to profile themselves as an elite sport city, for example by hosting major sports events such as marathons, European Championships and even the Giro d'Italia. Regional Olympic Support centres and Sports Medical Advice centres have also been given a place in local sports policies to support elite athletes. Even so, expenditure on elite sport amongst the five largest cities in the Netherlands is still limited to around €1 million per city.

Norway
Current sport structures

National government
Responsibility for sport in Norway is shared between the government (Ministry of Culture and Church Affairs) and non-governmental organizations, the former being primarily responsible for facilities and the latter for activities. The highest decision-making body in Norwegian sport is the General Assembly of Sports which sits for a term of four years. This consists of 75 representatives from 55 sport federations, 75 representatives from the district sport associations, 11 representatives from the NOC board, one Norwegian IOC representative, one athlete representative and one employee representative.

National Olympic Committee
Sport is the largest voluntary sector activity in Norway. The current NOC (formed in 1996 following an amalgamation of the Norwegian Olympic Committee and Confederation of Sports in 1996) is the umbrella national sports organisation in Norway, representing approximately 40% of the Norwegian population.

At the elite level, it is Olympiatoppen (a division of the NOC) which is responsible for elite sport in Norway. The forerunner of Olympiatoppen was founded after poor results during the Winter Olympics in 1984. Whereas Norway failed to win a gold medal in 1988, it won nine gold medals, six silver and five bronze four years later in Albertville (1992) and received additional funding in preparation for hosting the Lillehammer Games in 1994. Since the Sydney Olympics in 2000, Olympiatoppen has developed a range of sports science and medicine support services and is currently structured in four main units:

1   Professional development and guidance (research and development, health, nutrition, strength/power, technique/motor development, endurance, psychology, test/training)
2.   Coaching in high priority sports (endurance sports, technical sports and team sports),
3.   Athletes and coaches career development (coaches education, preparation for post- athletic career)
4.   Hotel operation

National governing bodies
The 55 sports federations and 19 district associations are primarily concerned with competitive sport and sport for all respectively. At the local level there are some 12,300 sports clubs, 5000 being company clubs.

Lotteries
Most of the money in Norwegian sport comes from the lotteries (Norsk Tipping): in 2003 approximately €130 million was distributed through the Ministry of Culture and Church Affairs. Half of this sum is allocated to the NOC and half is earmarked for facilities and for local sports clubs which can apply for funds to build facilities. As well as funding Olympiatoppen (approx €7 million in 2003), the NOC distributes funds to, among others, the national and district sports federations. Lottery funds account for 76% of the NOC's resources, the balance coming from sponsorship (20%) and sales (4%) (Enjolras 2002).

In Norway, the profit from lotteries is regarded as public money because the shareholding company "Norsk Tipping" is state-owned. Parliament determines what percentage of Lottery proceeds goes to sport (since 2002, sport has received a half, having previously received a third) and government determines how funds are distributed to the different sports organizations. Lottery funds for sport are passed directly to the Ministry rather than being held centrally within the Government budget.

Local government
Norway is divided into 19 counties which have responsibility for sport-related issues at the regional level. They assist municipalities in their work, especially during the planning and construction of sport facilities.

United Kingdom

Historical background

Although previously implicit in the "continuum" approach to sports policy (i.e. foundation, participation, performance and excellence), elite sport only truly achieved prominence as an official area of UK government policy in 1997 when funding from the Sports Lottery Fund was permitted to be used for revenue rather than capital funding purposes.

Prior to 1997, funding for "Performance and Excellence" programmes was limited and although sports administrators had an understanding of what was required to develop an elite sports programme, there were insufficient resources to fund such a programme to the fullest extent.

The performance of UK athletes in the Olympic Games of Atlanta 1996 was perceived to have been a disaster, with Team GB winning only 1 gold medal and finishing in 36th place in the medal table. Lottery criteria were changed in 1997 permitting funds to be used for selected revenue activities of which elite sport was an eligible area. Between 1997 and 2005 an average of around € 32 million per year has been invested in creating a world class system for elite sport in the UK. This money has supported governing bodies' World Class Performance Programmes and has also provided means-tested help for athletes via Athlete Personal Awards (average award per athlete in 2005: € 18,000 p.a.). Following the introduction of the WCPP there has been a dramatic improvement in GBR's performance in the Olympic Games with 11 gold medals and 10th place in Sydney 2000 followed by 9 gold medals and 10th place in Athens 2004.

National government

Central government responsibility for sport is part of the portfolio of the Department for Culture Media and Sport (DCMS) which was founded in 1992. The DCMS funds sport via Exchequer distributions to two Non-Departmental Public Bodies with a remit for sport – UK Sport and Sport England. UK Sport is the UK-wide body with a brief for elite sport, major sports events, anti doping, international relations and ethics. Technically central government provides funding for sport but policy is formulated on an 'arms length' basis.

At the same time, there has been a degree of political devolution to Scotland, Wales and Northern Ireland, arguably resulting in a greater sense of national identity. One of the ways in which this identity is expressed is through sport. Like England, Scotland, Wales and Northern Ireland, each has its own Sports Council. **sport**scotland, the Sports Council for Wales and Sport Northern Ireland are accountable respectively to the Scottish Parliament, the Welsh Assembly and the Northern Ireland Assembly. All three bodies have their own schemes for assisting "potential"-level and sub-elite athletes - some of whom will graduate to the UK-level World Class Programme. Sport England's responsibilities in this respect transferred to UK Sport on 1 April 2006. The four 'home nations' have all made separate investments in elite sport in order to achieve success in, for example, the Commonwealth Games.

Current sport structures

National governing bodies

The national governing bodies of sport are responsible for all formal participation in their sport at all levels. Until 2004, a governing body's ability to access funding from the World Class Performance Programme (or equivalent programmes in the Home Nation Sports Councils) was dependent on the preparation of an appropriate World Class Performance Plan (WCPP). In 2004, however, the Sports Councils collectively introduced the concept of the "One Stop Plan", designed to enable an initial group of sports to develop co-ordinated UK-wide plans covering the whole of the performance pathway - and to benefit from a simplified funding process.

The representative body for national governing bodies in England is the Central Council for Physical Recreation (CCPR). The CCPR and its equivalent bodies in Scotland, Wales and Northern Ireland lobby government on behalf of sport but do not have the same formal responsibility for sports policy as the Sports Councils.

National Olympic Committee (NOC)

The British Olympic Association (BOA) and the British Paralympic Association (BPA) are respectively the National Olympic Committee and the National Paralympic Committee for the UK. Their primary responsibility is the preparation of the UK team (officially called Great Britain & Northern Ireland) for both the Summer and Winter Olympic and Paralympic Games. Although UK Sport, the BOA and the BPA are separate bodies, they work closely in partnership.

Lotteries

Since 1994 there has been a National Lottery in the UK from which 28% of turnover is distributed to 'good causes'. Sport is recognised as a good cause and receives 16.7% of the allocation to good causes (i.e. 4.67% of total turnover). In the early years of the National Lottery receipts exceeded expectations leading to an annual disbursement of around € 400 million per year to sport. More recently National Lottery sales have fallen and annual disbursements for the short to medium term are anticipated to be in the € 300 million per year range.

Local government

Local authorities are the most significant funders and providers of sporting opportunities in the UK. However their remit for elite sport is limited. A number of local authorities have constructed sports facilities that can be used by elite athletes for training and competition purposes. Access to such facilities and other support facilities is a function of local policy and decision making – both of which are variable across authorities.

Media & commercial sector

The **media** supports elite sport in the UK indirectly via coverage in print media, television and radio broadcasting and increasingly the Internet.

Businesses support elite sport in an ad hoc manner. Individual athletes can receive funding in the form of endorsements and sponsorships. These financial arrangements are usually not in the public domain but provide a limited number of athletes with funding which they are able to use both as income and as a means to support their training and competition programmes. The BOA enjoys the support of a variety of commercial partners who contribute towards the funding of Team GB.

APPENDIX 4: TOTAL NATIONAL EXPENDITURE ON SPORT (2003)

	Total national expenditure on sport 2003		Total national expenditure on sport (per head of population)	Change in national expenditure on sport 1999-2003	Total Government expenditure on sport (% of total Government expenditure)	NOTES
CAN	€67.9m*	state: 69m*	€2.1	+68.5%	0.05%	*excludes government money (€2m p.a.) allocated by the Ministry of Health for physical activity; furthermore, Provinces in Canada also invest in elite sport, like in Quebec 3.7 million is spent directly to support elite athletes; there is no national lottery money for sport in Canada (Copps, 2004)
FLA	€71,9m	state: 64.4m Lotteries 7.5m	€12.04	+72.8%	0.32%	* includes government money to Bloso (62.7) and the department youth and sport (1.7m). Lottery funding to Bloso: 5,63m) and lottery funding to the BOIC (1.86m) * the total national budget in 2003 was €85.6m, of which Bloso has € 75.2 m, BOIC €5.9 m and the Ministry Youth and Sport: €4.4mS
IT	€273.7m	state: 127.7m lotteries: 146m (2002)	€4.7	-26.6%	0.02%	includes expenditure on sports facilities (€1.5m) and payments made to nine military clubs (€1.2m) that employ top level athletes and coaches
NL	€127.2m	state: 79.2m lotteries: 43m	€7.8	+98.8%	0.06%	excludes local expenditure on sport (esp. on sports facilities) which come to €1040 million (gross) or €765 million (the net including receipts from these facilities)
NOR	€130m	state/Lotteries:* 130m	€28.4	+30.8%	0.17%	Government expenditure on sport is derived in full from the national lottery (Norsk Tipping: €130m p.a.), of which €65m is allocated to NOC and €65m directly to sports facilities
UK	€610m	state: 350m* lotteries: 260m	€10.1	+45%	0.05%	*includes government money (€150m p.a.) allocated by the Dept for Education & Skills for specialist sports colleges and school sport coordinators.
WAL	40.8	Adeps: 17.0 (from government + lotteries)	9.3 (€4.4)	4	NA	

APPENDIX 5: TOTAL NATIONAL EXPENDITURE ON ELITE SPORT (2003)

	National expenditure on elite sport 2003	National expenditure on elite sport (per head of population)	Change in national expenditure on elite sport 1999-2003	National expenditure on elite sport (% of total national expenditure on sport)	REMARKS
CAN	€38.1m	€1.17	NA	56.1%	Includes: state: €28.1, COC: €8.1m, Lotteries: €1.88m
FL	€8.4m	€1.41	+115%*	11.7%	*includes Bloso (expenditures only for elite sport purposes), BOIC (2/3 of total budget for Flanders) and department youth and Sport (Ministry of Sport)
IT	€125m (estimated)*	€2.15 (estimated)	NA	45.7%	Although NOC (CONI) allocates €25m direct to elite sport, it is not known what proportion of the money it allocates to NGBs is spent on elite sport programmes. Neither is it known what proportion of lottery funds are used for elite sport purposes;
NL	€41.6	€2.6	+54%	32.7%	
NOR	€7m*	€1.53	+27.2%	5.4%	84% of the budget of Olympiatoppen derives from government and 16% from sponsors; in 2006 the total budget of Olympiatoppen was € 9.6m.
UK	€90.3m*	€1.5	+126.8%	14.8%	Excludes: - awards made by the English, Scottish, Welsh and Northern Irish Sports Councils for junior/sub-elite level athletes - awards made for the bidding for and staging of major international sports events - UK Sport operational costs
WAL	€3.8m	€0.87	+82.5%	9.3%	

APPENDIX 6: FINANCIAL SUPPORT FOR NATIONAL GOVERNING BODIES (2003)

	CAN	FL	IT	NL	NOR	UK	Wall.
Number of recognised & funded **NGBs**	55	68	77 (= 43 federations + 18 associated disciplines + 16 enti di promozione sportive)	72	55	120*	64
Total funding of NGBs	€27.5m*	€22.8m	€140m	€65.7m	€19m	€95m**	9
Funding per head of population	€0.85m	€3.82m	€2.41m	€4.03m	€4.15m	€1.6m	2.00
Average funding per NGB	€0.5m	€0.34m	€1.82m	€0.91mj	€0.35m	€0.79m	0.14
Number of NGBs funded for elite sport purposes	47**	26	41	63	30	40***	36
Total funding of NGBs for elite sport purposes	€18	€5.7m*	€25.1m**	€31	€4m	€50m****	3.81
Elite sport funding (% of total funding)	65.45%	25.0%	17.86%	47.18%	21.05%	52.6%	42.33
Average funding (elite sport) per NGB	€0.38m	€0.22m	€0.61m	€0.49	€0.13m	€1.25m	0.11
Notes	* Mainly from Sport Canada (government); also Olympic Committee. Coaching Association Canada	* Bloso funding only: figure does not include any funding provided by BOIC		* In 2003, 55 NGB's were entitled to special elite funds because their disciplines fall within what in the Netherlands are defined as 'category 1 or 2 elite sport disciplines'. However, in 2003 also other NGB's received funds from either the central government or the lotteries for elite sport purposes (65 in total).		* This number will include for some sports, separate governing bodies for England, Scotland, Wales and Northern Ireland ** all sports Councils: UK Sport, Sport England, Sport Scotland, Sport Wales, Northern Ireland *** these are a subset of the estimated 120 NSOs who receive funding for various purposes from one or more of the UK's five Sports Councils. **** figure excluding: 1) awards made to NSFs by the home country Sports Councils in respect of young and/or emerging athletes who currently do not qualify for their World Class Performance Programme or similar 2) any awards made to NSFs by the Sports Councils in respect of the bidding and staging of major international sports events	

APPENDIX 7: FINANCIAL SUPPORT FOR ATHLETES

	Financial support	**Number of athletes receiving support (2003)**
Canada	Wage for living and finance for training: 1053 Euros a month. Students: 632 Euro/month Criterion: athletes all ready or having the potential to be top 16 in the world	N.A.
Flanders	Employment contract (since 1995) on average € 19,294 Euros a year (€ 1,608 a month) (depending on diploma) + reimbursements. This contract is a GESCO statute, subject to low taxes and is subsidised by the ministry of employment Criterion: approximately top 12 in the world	36 (42 places available)
Italy	On average € 15,000 a year + retirement fund. Furthermore money for Olympic medals is € 130,000 for gold, € 65,000 for silver and 40,000 for bronze Criterion: depending on the sport, determined by NGB and NOC)	400
The Netherlands	Stipends in the Netherlands: 70% of the minimum wage, on average 956 euros a month, in 2003 54% of all A-athletes; in 2005 56% of all A-athletes +reimbursements for A- and B-athletes for sport-related costs, with an upper limit of € 455 per month (€ 5,460 a year) for A-athletes and € 137 per month (€ 1,644 a year) for B-athletes. Additional services, like a car (only) for A-athletes, as part of sponsor contracts of NOC*NSF and its 'Partners in Sport'. Criterion: top 8 in the world for A-athletes; having participated to European Championships for B-athletes	360 athletes
Norway	Payments are based on performances A- athletes: max.€ 12,000 Euros/year B- athletes: max.€ 6,000 Euros/year U (development): max. 6,000 Euros/year Team: 6,000 Euros/year for each participant The budget goes to the NGB who decides whether this goes directly to the athlete or to invest it in costs, like training camps Criterion: not known, depending on the sport	60 70 (20) 40
United Kingdom	On average 15,992 Euros a year (€ 1,333 a month) Ranging from € 2,900 to € 29,000) Criterion: top 20 in the world (individual sports) and top 10 in the world (team sports)	525 athletes
Wallonia	Employment contracts, since 1999. Exact amount is not known. According to the decree of 1999 the NGB decides on this.	18 athletes (2003)

APPENDIX 8: RADAR GRAPHS FOR OTHER SAMPLE NATIONS BASED ON TABLE 6.3

Italy

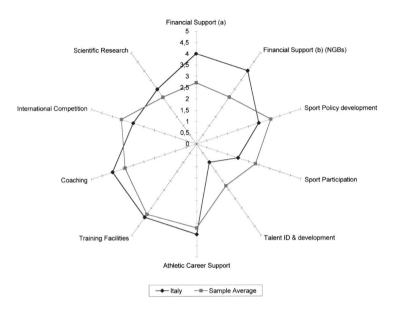

The Netherlands

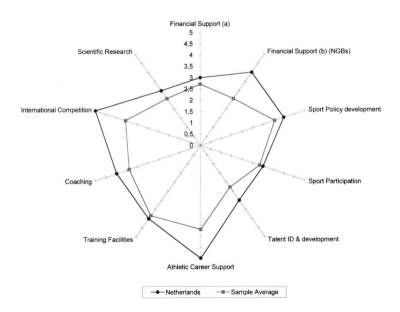

Canada

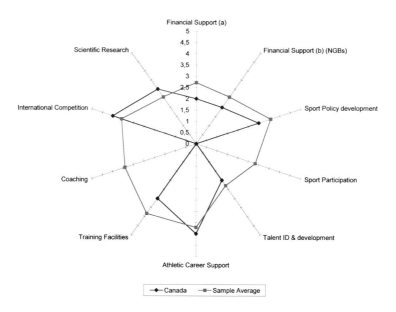

Norway

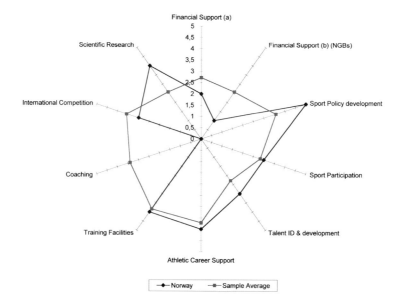

Wallonia

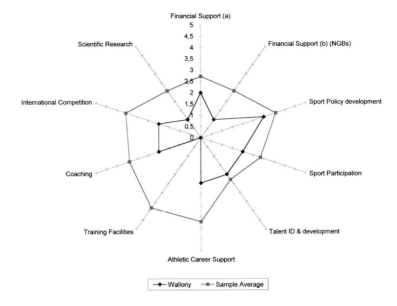

Additional

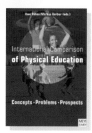

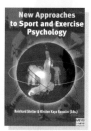

Gershon Tenenbaum/
Marcy Driscoll
**Methods of Research in
Sport Sciences –
Quantitative and
Qualitative Approaches**
A Handbook

G. Spitzer (Ed.)
**Doping and
Doping Control in
Europe**

Uwe Pühse/
Markus Gerber (eds.)
**International
Comparison of Physical
Education**
Concepts, Problems,
Prospects

Reinhard Stelter/
Kirsten Kaya Roessler
**New Approaches to Sport
and Exercise Psychology**

776 pages
140 illustrations, 60 charts
Paperback, 6^1/2" x 9^1/4"
ISBN: 978-1-84126-133-1
$ 59.95 US/$ 89.95 CDN
£ 39.95 UK/€ 49.90

210 pages
8 tables
Paperback, 5^3/4" x 8^1/4"
ISBN: 978-1-84126-215-4
$ 19.95 US/$ 29.95 CDN
£ 14.95 UK/€ 18.95

720 pages
Full-color print, 123 photos
101 illustrations, 80 tables
Hardcover, 5^3/4" x 8^1/4"
ISBN: 978-1-84126-161-7
$ 75.00 US/$ 119.95 CDN
£ 49.95 UK/€ 59.95

192 pages
5 photos, 15 illustrations
Paperback, 6^1/2" x 9^1/4"
ISBN: 978-1-84126-149-2
$ 19.95 US/$ 29.95 CDN
£ 14.95 UK/€ 18.90

Volume 1+2
Gudrun Doll-Tepper/Michael Kröner/Werner
Sonnenschein (eds.)
New Horizons in Sport for Athletes with a Disability

Proceedings of the International Vista '99 Conference
German Sport University Cologne, 28 Aug. – 1 Sep. 1999

Zsolt Radak (ed.)
Exercise and Diseases
Prevention through Training

Ken Hardman/
Joy Standeven (eds.)
**Cultural Diversity
and Congruence in Physical
Education and Sport**
ISCPES-Proceedings
Hachi-ohji-Conference
Japan 1996

Paperback, 5^3/4" x 8^1/4"
Vol. 1: 488 pages, 90 figures, 28 tables,
ISBN: 978-1-84126-036-5
Vol. 2: 480 pages, 32 figures, 19 tables,
ISBN: 978-1-84126-037-2
$ 29.00 US/$ 39.95 CDN
£ 17.95 UK/€ 23.90 per volume

190 pages
15 illustrations, 11 tables
Paperback, 5^3/4" x 8^1/4"
ISBN: 978-1-84126-121-8
$ 17.95 US/$ 25.95 CDN
£ 12.95 UK/€ 18.90

360 pages
23 figures, 28 tables
Paperback, 5^3/4" x 8^1/4"
ISBN: 978-3-89124-557-6
$ 29.00 US/$ 39.95 CDN
£ 17.95 UK/€ 23.90

MEYER
& MEYER
SPORT

The Sports Publisher

MEYER & MEYER Sport | www.m-m-sports.com | sales@m-m-sports.com

Scientific Titles:

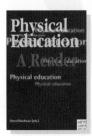

Ken Hardman/
Ken Green (eds.)
**Physical Education:
A Reader**

3rd edition
382 pages
11 tables
Paperback, 5$^3/4$" x 8$^1/4$"
ISBN: 978-1-84126-027-3
$ 29.00 US/$ 39.95 CDN
£ 17.95 UK/€ 23.90

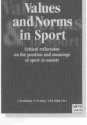

Johan Steenbergen/
P. De Knop/
A.H.F Elling (eds.)
Values & Norms in Sport
Critical Reflections
on the Position and
Meanings
of Sport in Society

376 pages
13 tables, 1 figure
Paperback, 5$^3/4$" x 8$^1/4$"
ISBN: 978-1-84126-057-0
$ 24.00 US/$ 34.95 CDN
£ 17.95 UK/€ 23.90

Walter Tokarski/
Dirk Steinbach/
Karen Petry/Barbara Jesse
Two Players One Goal?
Sport in the European Union

288 pages
48 illustrations
Paperback, 5$^3/4$" x 8$^1/4$"
ISBN: 978-1-84126-092-1
$ 19.95 US/$ 29.95 CDN
£ 14.95 UK/€ 18.90

TAFISA/
Lamartine DaCosta/
Ana M. Miragaya (eds.)
**Worldwide Experiences
and Trends in Sport for All**

2nd edition
792 pages
37 figures, 139 tables
Hardcover, 5$^3/4$" x 8$^1/4$"
ISBN: 978-1-84126-085-3
$ 58.00 US/$ 79.95 CDN
£ 40.00 UK/€ 65.90

Müller/Bacharach/
Klika/Lindinger/
Schwameder (eds.)
Science and Skiing III

440 pages
45 photos and 187
illustrations
Paperback, 5$^3/4$" x 8$^1/4$"
ISBN: 978-1-84126-177-5
$ 29.00 US/$ 39.95 CDN
£ 17.95 UK/€ 23.90

Jan Tolleneer/
Roland Renson (eds.)
**Old Borders,
New Borders,
No Borders**
Sport and Physical
Education in a Period of
Change

440 pages
26 figures, 48 tables
Paperback, 5$^3/4$" x 8$^1/4$"
ISBN: 978-1-84126-052-5
$ 29.00 US/$ 39.95 CDN
£ 17.95 UK/€ 23.90

The Business of Sports,
Volume 1
James Skinner/
Allan Edwards
The Sport Empire

192 pages
3 charts
Paperback, 6$^1/2$" x 9$^1/4$"
ISBN: 978-1-84126-168-3
$ 19.95 US/$ 29.95 CDN
£ 14.95 UK/€ 18.95

The Business of Sports,
Volume 2
Annelies Knoppers/
Anton Anthonissen (Eds.)
**Making Sense of Diversity
in Organizing Sport**

120 pages
2 charts
Paperback, 6$^1/2$" x 9$^1/4$"
ISBN: 978-1-84126-203-1
$ 19.95 US/$ 29.95 CDN
£ 14.95 UK/€ 18.95

The Sports Publisher

MEYER
& MEYER
SPORT

MEYER & MEYER Sport | www.m-m-sports.com | sales@m-m-sports.com

Photo & Illustration Credits

Cover Photos: Belga; gymfed
Cover Design: Jens Vogelsang
Photos: Belga; gymfed
                 getty images: 85, 89, 121, 163, 166